HOW TO BECOME THE PERSON YOU WANT TO BE

STRATEGIES FOR TAKING CONTROL OF YOUR FUTURE

SOME THINGS TO THINK ABOUT - FOR YOUNG PEOPLE
(AND THOSE WHO CARE ABOUT THEM)

LARRY SHIRER
2024

HOW TO BECOME THE PERSON YOU WANT TO BE

STRATEGIES FOR TAKING CONTROL OF YOUR FUTURE

Copyright 2024 by Larry Shirer

All Rights Reserved

No part of this publication may be reproduced, stored or transmitted in any form or by any means: electronic, mechanical, digital, photocopy, recording, or any other- except for brief quotations in printed reviews, without permission from the publisher.

ISBN Print 979-8-9891882-4-6

ISBN Ebook 979-8-9891882-5-3

Printed in USA

First Edition 2024

Author's Web Site: larrysbooksandphotos.com

Author's email: lshirer@sssnet.com

DEDICATION

This book is dedicated to my grandchildren, their children, and their grandchildren.

CONTENTS

INTRODUCTION	1
PART I. - FOUNDATIONS	**5**
1. Values	5
2. Principles	9
3. Character	11
PART II. - SOME DECISIONS SHAPE YOUR LIFE	**43**
4. Nurture Personal Relationships	43
5. Exclude Some Things From Your Life	72
PART III. - HOW TO MAKE BETTER DECISIONS	**94**
6. Choices Matter	94
7. Develop An Effective Decision-Making Process	98
PART IV. - CONSIDER YOUR PERSPECTIVES	**123**
8. Examine Your Worldview	123
9. Consider Humankind's Relationship To Nature	131
PART V. - STRATEGIES FOR TAKING CONTROL OF YOUR FUTURE	**134**
10. Examine Your Attitudes	134
11. Make Things Happen	149
PART VI. - PULL IT ALL TOGETHER	**170**
12. Develop A Purpose	170
13. Develop Life Goals and Objectives	173
14. Develop A Personal Mission Statement	185
PART VII. - CHOOSE TO MAKE YOUR LIFE MEANINGFUL	**187**
15. Choose To Be A Better You	187

| 16. | Let Your Life Speak | 189 |
| 17. | Choose To Really Live | 190 |

APPENDICES	194
BIBLIOGRAPHY	224
ABOUT THE AUTHOR	227

INTRODUCTION

Choices matter! Individual decisions, the choices you make, literally determine the course and quality of your life. Who you are, what you do, your mental and emotional state, and what you will become, all depend largely upon the **decisions** you make. Your happiness, success, health, achievements, morality and the extent to which your life has meaning are determined primarily by the quality of your decisions. In turn, the quality of your decisions is determined by your **values, principles, and character**.

If you are interested in making effective decisions about the many forces and pressures that affect your life, if you are ready to take responsible control of your life, the information, guidelines, tips and strategies offered here can help.

Dealing effectively with life requires that you; <u>understand the Way Things Are,</u> and <u>decide Which Things Matter.</u>

Young people are forced to deal with many choices. Some are difficult and have long term implications. Some can be confusing, even un-nerving. Thinking about decision making, developing relevant skills, and preparing yourself for making effective choices will help improve the results of your decisions, and your life. Carefully selecting values and principles, and determining the kind of character you want, increases the odds that you will be able to choose effectively.

The world is confusing. Every day you are forced to make choices about how to live your life. Ideally your choices should be consistent with your values. For that to be real and effective, you must decide what values are important to you.

You have access to huge amounts of information and many options. You are required, (by design or default), to choose: values, principles, goals and objectives, careers, where to reside, a spouse, (or not to have one), a worldview, what personal philosophy and religion to embrace, (or to embrace none), how to relate to people, and more. You are bombarded with the need to make choices. How well you cope depends on how clearly you think.

Today's young people are confronted with many more choices than those of previous generations. The pressures can be staggering. I get that. The world is different than when I was young. I get that. There are, however, time and experience tested values and principles that will help you deal with the pressures.

We make lots of decisions. The only thing we do more than make decisions is breathe. Aristotle, a respected Greek philosopher, observed long ago that "we become what we are as persons by the decisions that we make." That truth hasn't changed. The quality of our lives is determined by the decisions we make.

There are a few fundamental decisions that shape our lives. In this book, we will discuss several:

- Who do I choose to be?
- How do I choose to see the world?
- How shall I live my life?
- What should I exclude from my life?
- How should I relate to other people?
- How will I contribute to family and community?
- What's it all about?

There is no one set of answers to these questions that is "right" for everyone, but there are principles and values that make some choices more effective than others. It's worth your effort to seriously think about, and carefully select, the standards by which you will live your life.

The book is organized into seven parts. After this brief introduction, Part I provides an overview of the importance of Values, Principles, and Character, how to choose and develop these standards for living, and how to build a virtuous character. Part II focuses on two of the critical decisions that shape your life. Part III outlines a process for making better decisions. Part IV helps you examine your perspectives about how the world works. Part V offers some strategies for taking control of your life. Part VI outlines a process for pulling everything together into a plan. Part VII suggests ways to make your life effective, satisfying, and meaningful.

In addition to suggestions about values, principles, character, and strategies for becoming the person you want to be, the text includes "case studies", examples, and exercises to help clarify the concepts discussed.

One of the fundamental choices you must make is about who is going to be in **control** of your life. Will it be authority figures, your peers, or you? Occasionally factors and events beyond our control significantly impact our lives. Things happen to us. But, to a much greater extent than we often admit, we mold our lives and control our futures through the decisions we make. Other people make decisions that affect you, but you can always choose your response, and thus determine what happens next. Practical strategies for taking responsible control of your own life are critical components of the text.

If you will read, think about, and implement the tips and strategies outlined in this book, it will help you:

- Clarify the values that are important to you.
- Identify useful principles to guide your life.
- Determine the kind of character you want to build, and how to develop it.

- Understand how the world works.
- Determine what matters.
- Build better personal relationships.
- Deal with peer pressure.
- Make better decisions more consistently.
- Exercise more control over your life.
- Develop a purpose, mission and plan for your life.

This is not a book of does and don'ts. It's a book about THINKING and DECIDING. I can't make you do anything. I will supply information, identify alternatives, describe some tools and techniques, and indicate some pros and cons. The CHOICES are yours.

PART I - FOUNDATIONS

Values, principles and character define who you are. They are the building blocks upon which a life is built.

CHAPTER 1 - VALUES

Values – An Overview

We humans have been blessed with the extraordinary power of choice - free will. Whether we are aware of it or not, our choices are determined by our values. Values are those personal standards for living that we deem to have inherent worth and which we consider deeply important. Values define our essence, our uniqueness, what really matters to us. Values shape decisions and decisions shape lives.

Our real values, however, are often not what we profess them to be, but are defined by the choices we make in our interactions with others. Our values define how we distinguish right and wrong, good and bad. Answers which are the easiest, the most convenient, or the most personally beneficial are not always the "right" decisions. Choices, which are effective and with which you can live comfortably, must be consistent with your core values. If your behavior is not consistent with your values, you will feel dissatisfied with the results, uncomfortable, and out of sync with the world. When your actions are consistent with your values, you are much more likely to achieve positive outcomes and be more satisfied with your choices.

Decisions about personal values are some of the most important decisions you ever make. They determine the kind of person you become. Once established, they should serve as guides for making other important decisions. They form the foundation on which your life is built.

Your values should provide an internal compass that guides your life journey. To determine if a decision is "right", <u>you should test possible choices against your values</u>. To test a decision against your values, you must have previously considered and defined your ethical and moral standards, and what core values are really important to you. That requires careful thought and is something that should be done with deliberation and great care. When faced with a decision in times of pressure, crisis, or change, having decided ahead of time what is important will mean you are better prepared to <u>align your actions with your values</u>.

With every decision you make, you are writing the story of your life. Choosing the right values will give your life story meaning, and make it something of which you can be proud.

It is important to understand that values have the following attributes:

1. Values are individualized. Each person has a different list and different priorities within that list.
2. Everyone has a set of values whether or not they are specifically identified.
3. Most of us live our lives with core values established by others. We adopt them from authority figures, peers, and culture, without making conscious decisions about them.
4. Defining your values help you make better choices.
5. Values determine your priorities.
6. Values are measurements useful for determining if your life is turning out like you want it to be.
7. Values are not static. They may change as you learn and grow.
8. Keeping in touch with your values should be a lifelong exercise. You should frequently revisit them, especially if you start to feel unbalanced or uncertain.

Basic values such as integrity/honesty are critical. When deciding which values are important to you, consider the following questions:

- How do I decide if an action is right or wrong?
- What kind of person do I want to be?
- What do I consider to be my moral absolutes?
- How do I make decisions about how I should treat people?
- How do I want to be treated?
- What do I consider to be my basic personal responsibilities?
- What are the qualities I admire about people I respect?
- What makes me feel fulfilled and proud?
- What values were involved in decisions I regret?

Don't let the past steal your present and future. If you are not satisfied with your life, you can change it. The critical first step in change is to clarify your values.

Values help you make choices about what is right and wrong and what is the responsible thing to do under the circumstances. Selecting and living your values makes you the author of your life.

Appendix A, (at the back of the book), contains a list of the values most commonly mentioned when people are asked about such things. Please go there to select the values you consider the most important for guiding your decisions. Select the 15-24 you consider the most important.

Reflect on your selections for a few days. When you are satisfied with your choices, prioritize the list into three categories using the worksheet in Appendix B. Ranking values in one priority list can be difficult. Placing them in three categories encourages you to really think about them and will help in circumstances where values may appear to be in conflict.

Periodically reflect on how consistently you are living your chosen values. If you determine that your decisions do not match your values, decide if you need to change your values or change your decisions.

CHAPTER 2 – PRINCIPLES

Principles – An Overview

A life of meaning and satisfaction is based, not on material wealth, but on living a life aligned with the right principles. Principles are the value based standards we use to decide how to act and react. Principles are matters of personal choice. Valid principles are not rules developed by a committee, but are derived from the experiences of what has worked best for our species over our history. They represent the time and experience tested collective wisdom of humankind. Principles seldom change.

Principles are decision guidelines that one uses to make decisions about how to live. Their purpose is to align one's behavior with one's ideals. They are typically declarative, expressed in "I will" or "I will not" statements. Sound principles are based on concepts that reflect human decency and effectiveness.

Effective principles are related to, and derived from, sound values, e.g. the principles - "I will not lie, cheat or steal" are based upon the value of – honesty/integrity. The principle of being helpful to those with physical and emotional difficulties derives from the value of compassion.

A principle is a fundamental truth or proposition that serves as the foundation for a system of belief or behavior, or for a chain of reasoning. Principles are codes of conduct.

Principles are the foundation of human behavior. They are concepts on which to build a life. They determine the difference between what you are today and what you could be.

Personal principles originate from one's perceptions of how the world works and one's personal objectives. In other words, personal principles are formed by what you have learned, your thinking, your perspectives, your values, your experiences, the results you have observed, and the results you hope to achieve.

Whether we believe it or not, we live in a world that is governed by principles and laws.

Principles have important benefits:

- Principles improve the effectiveness of decision making by helping us keep our behavior in line with our values. They help us determine the "right" thing to do in light of the existing circumstances.
- Principles reduce stress and time spent in decision making because we have thought through and decided what to do when faced with various circumstances.
- Principles help us determine and understand our reasons for doing what we do.
- By centering our lives on timeless, valid principles we create a pattern for effective living.

Principles are the value based standards we use to decide how to act and how to react to what comes up. Principles are decision guidelines that we choose, and then use, to make decisions about how to live.

There should be a direct link between your values and your principles. To help you understand the connection, Appendix C provides a number of principle statements that are directly related to some of the most common values.

To develop principles that reflect the values you have selected, please list the values you chose for your life in the left-hand column in Appendix D. In the right-hand column, write in a logical, and related, "I will or I will not" statement that reflects the value.

Values and principles define character, which we will look at next.

CHAPTER 3 – CHARACTER

I have a dream that my four little children will one day live in a nation where they will not be judged by the color of their skin, but by the content of their characters.

Do you recognize these words? They are, of course, from the "I Have a Dream" speech by Martin Luther King, Jr., delivered in Washington, DC, on August 28, 1963. It marked a pivotal day in the Civil Rights Movement, and is regarded by many as one of the greatest speeches ever delivered.

King obviously thought that character is important. He dreamed of a day when his children, (and by implication, all people), would be judged by the content of their characters. It is a worthy dream, for us all, and highlights the importance of character.

A. Character – An Overview

Personal character is defined by consciously and consistently living one's values and principles. One's character can range from evil, to ambivalent, to virtuous, depending on the values and principles chosen.

The word character comes from the Greek word **kharakter**, meaning "to engrave." Our character is composed of the values and principles that have become engraved in us, so that they determine how we act when faced with choices, and how we react to experiences.

Character determines self-respect and the respect with which we are regarded by others. Character is determined by how we resolve the inner conflict between what is self-serving and what is right. Personal values and principles are the foundations, the determinants, of character.

Character development, the transition from a preoccupation with self, to consciousness of, and caring for others, is an important element of personal growth. Your character defines who you are as a person. Character determines how you respond to the events and circumstances in your life. How you respond determines the results of those encounters.

> *What lies behind us and what lies before us are small matters compared to what lies within us.*
> - Ralph Waldo Emerson

One's worth as an individual is determined by character, not by titles, educational degrees, possessions, or wealth. To some extent, character is influenced by genes, experiences, examples, and education, but it is largely determined by judgment, discretion, and personal choices. Character is malleable - we get to choose which traits we want to develop and emphasize. Our "self" is elastic. We can mold it if we so choose. A person of "strong" character is one who is moral and ethical, does what is right in spite of personal gain or hardship, cares about people, and can be trusted.

Character defines who you are. In the final analysis, who you <u>are</u> determines the worth, the effectiveness, of your life, and communicates what you value much more accurately than anything you say. Your character is defined by the principles by which you conduct your life. Many generations from multiple cultures have demonstrated that there are basic **principles** for living effectively, and that people can be truly successful and happy only if they learn to integrate those principles into their basic characters.

The shaping of character is based upon the fundamental idea that there are certain principles that govern human decency and effectiveness, natural laws in the human dimension that are just as real as natural laws in the physical dimension, (such as the law of gravity).

Your character is your identity. Make your character one of which you are proud.

Please read and think about the story in Case Study 1, "Learning from Bad Experiences," at the end of this chapter.

(Before reflecting on any of the case studies, please read the Note About Using Case Studies in Appendix E).

Character is engraved by how we chose to handle experiences, and what we learn from them. Character is never static. It evolves over time. Every choice, every action, adds or subtracts from one's character.

Character matters. It determines who and what you are as a person. It is a major determinant of the quality of your life, your happiness and "success."

B. Attributes of a Virtuous Character

The following are many of the attributes/traits that have been identified as elements of a strong character:

1. **Morality & Ethics** - Not all decisions involve moral choices. Choosing the restaurant for lunch is morally neutral. Others, such as decisions about whether to lie, cheat or steal, can have profound consequences. Those that force us to consider what is "right and wrong" can be challenging.

   So, I think ethics is a broader thing that's less focused on prohibitions and is more about looking at principles, questions and ideas about how to live your life.
   - Peter Singer

The basic standard is to treat others as you want to be treated. Albert Schweitzer elaborated on this theme by saying:

A man is truly ethical only when he obeys the compulsion to help all life which he is able to assist, and shrinks from injuring anything that lives.

2. **Honesty/Integrity** – This means not cheating, lying or stealing. Honesty is the foundation for trust, which is essential to cooperation and interpersonal relationships.

    Integrity is congruence between what you know, what you profess, and what you do.
    - Nathaniel Branden

    The first president of our country valued honesty.

    I hope I shall possess firmness and virtue enough to maintain what I consider the most enviable of all titles, the character of an honest man. - George Washington

    Please read and reflect on Case Study 2, "A Calculus Puzzle," at the end of this chapter.

3. **True/Truth** – We typically think of true as the opposite of false, and truth as the opposite of a lie. While these understandings are accurate, they are not complete. The concepts are multi-dimensional. Certainly, we should speak only the truth. What we say reflects what we are. Lying is destructive to relationships, and dishonest. Statements, contentions, and facts cannot be both true and false, as those of us who have taken true or false quizzes in school can attest. But there's more to the concepts:

- True can mean straight, or perfectly square, as in what a carpenter constructing a door frame aims to do, so that the door will open and close properly. A carpenter may use a "plumb bob" or a "square" to determine what is "true." It is unfortunate that we don't have such a tool for telling us if what we hear and read is "true."
- True can mean "real", as in; he is a "true" friend.
- True can mean "exemplary," as in; he is a "true" gentleman.
- True can mean "demonstrable," as in; ice melts at temperatures above 32 degrees F.
- True can mean "actual" as opposed to imaginary; as in: "true story" publications.
- True can mean "valuable," "meaningful," or "useful," when referring to the message in a story that is not necessarily factual.

Black Elk, a famous and oft quoted Sioux Medicine Man, when commenting upon one of the myths of his people, stated:

...this they tell, and whether it happened or not, I do not know, but if you think about it, you will see that it is true.

All of these dimensions of truth have relevance to how we live our lives. Living truthfully means not telling lies, but much more. It means being true to who we want to be and what we want to do. We should be true, be real, to others, but more importantly, we should be true to ourselves, true to our values and to what we "know" is right.

I prefer to be true to myself, even at the hazard of incurring the ridicule of others, rather than be false, and to incur my own abhorrence. – William Frederick Douglass

What is true for us may change. The world changes. We change. What was true for us at age 10 is not the same as what is true for us at age 80. That is not a bad thing. It is inevitable. We've had more experiences, learned more. Our circumstances have changed.

Socrates, the famous Greek philosopher, urged that we should ask ourselves three questions before making a statement: Is it **true?** Is it good? Is it useful?

Seek the truth. Think it through.

Please read and think about the situation in Case Study 3 – "In Want of a Signature," at the end of this chapter.

4. **Respect for Human Dignity** – We should embrace the concept that all persons have intrinsic worth and certain "unalienable rights," which we must honor if we expect to enjoy those same rights.

5. **Empathy and Compassion** - People matter. We should be ever aware of the impact of our actions, words and decisions on others. Empathy is a feeling. Compassion encompasses action. Almost all our decisions affect other people. We should treat people with dignity and respect, and seek to help with problems. Things are to be used. People are to be loved. Loving things and using people inevitably leads to poor consequences. We should understand that part of our "reason for being" is to help lighten the burdens of others.

6. **Kindness** – The attribute of kindness encompasses being attentive, considerate, generous, empathetic and friendly. It involves listening to and helping others. It means celebrating the successes of others and sharing their woes. It is an interpersonal skill that engenders trust and strengthens relationships. It means showing others in a multitude of little ways that you care.

Constant kindness can accomplish much. As the sun makes ice to melt, kindness causes misunderstanding, mistrust and hostility to evaporate.
   - Albert Schweitzer

7. **Responsibility** - No matter how good or bad our decisions, we are responsible for the consequences. We are responsible for our thoughts, beliefs, values, words, choices, and actions. We are responsible for how we treat other people, for keeping our promises, for our lives, and personal well-being. Blaming others or finding excuses does not change that reality. Recognizing and accepting personal responsibility will enable you to make better decisions.

    Being responsible requires self-discipline and effective time management. It means being conscientious, mindful, accountable and dependable. We should be particularly conscious of what we say, for words can wound deeper than a knife. We must accept that we have control. If we don't do something, nothing is going to get better. We must choose not to be victims. We should not, as many do, blame our circumstances on someone else's actions, or on the "system." Accepting responsibility is the first step to finding solutions.

    We should avoid falling into the trap of blaming someone or circumstances for our actions, as in: "I wouldn't have done that if she hadn't" ..., or, "He (or the devil) made me do it." We shouldn't offer lame excuses: "I felt hurt, so I ...", "I felt angry, so I ...", or, "I felt afraid, so I ..." or, "I couldn't help it." We have choices about how we respond to circumstances and the actions of others. We are responsible for our feelings and our actions.

We must be pro-active, avoiding the mindset of "Why doesn't someone do something?" Instead we should ask "What should I do?" Then do something.

We need to forego any feelings of entitlement. A journalist for *TIME* magazine characterized this "entitlement" attitude, embraced by far too many, as follows: "If I want it, I need it. If I need it, I have a right to it. If I have a right to it, someone owes it to me." The concept of accepting responsibility is contrary to the idea of entitlement.

The respect and trust of persons who we respect and trust are valuable assets. We earn that respect and trust by being competent and accountable, and by accepting responsibility for our actions.

We are each responsible for who we are, what we do, what we say, how we treat people, and how we live our lives. We are responsible for the consequences of our decisions. Accept personal responsibility.

> *People are always blaming their circumstances for what they are. I don't believe in circumstances. The people who get on in this world are the people who get up and look for the circumstances they want, and if they can't find them, make them.*
> \- George Bernard Shaw

In his book, *TAKING RESPONSIBILITY*, Nathaniel Branden, a PhD psychologist, suggests that we start each day with two questions: "What's good in my life?", and "What needs to be done?" The first question keeps us focused on the positives. The second reminds us that our lives and well-being are our own responsibility and keeps us proactive.

8. **Conscientiousness** - Studies have shown that conscientiousness is one of the traits shared by those who

attain high achievement and happiness.

> *Conscientiousness is emerging as one of the primary determinants of successful functioning across the lifespan.*
> — Paul Tough

> *Good luck is the willing handmaiden of an upright character and the conscientious observance of duty.*
> — James Russell Lowell

Being conscientious also means caring about the quality of what one does. We do not have to be perfect or do things perfectly, but setting high standards and striving to meet them leads to greater satisfaction and achievement, and earns the respect of others.

Be conscientious. It will help you fulfill your responsibilities to others and enhance how you feel about yourself and what you do.

> *Being conscientious is like brushing your teeth. It prevents problems.*
> — Brent Roberts

9. **Self-Control** – Means being rational and refusing to allow emotions to control your actions.

10. **Fairness/Justice** - Fairness is the principle upon which our whole system of justice is based and the foundation for our understanding of what is "right." Fairness involves treating everyone equitably and ensuring that everyone is given equal opportunity. Justice is the principle upon which right relationships are built.

11. **Quality/Excellence** - Whatever you do, attempt to do it well. Perfection is not possible, but striving for perfection makes a difference. (A word of caution about this advice, attributed to Bill Murray, the actor)

> *Whatever you do, give it 100%, unless you are donating blood.*
> - Bill Murray

12. **Do No Harm** – The most basic principle of all is that of not harming others. It includes not attempting to control or manipulate others, not trying to manage their affairs.

13. **Meet Commitments** – Demonstrating that you always do what you say you will do earns you the trust and respect of others and a clear conscience. Failing to meet commitments betrays others and yourself.

> *Resolve to perform what you ought; perform without fail what you resolve.*
> - Benjamin Franklin

14. **Courage** - Courage is sometimes defined as facing danger without fear. That is nonsense. Fear can be a useful emotion. Somewhere along the line it probably kept one of your ancestors alive. Ignoring fear in the face of danger is foolish. Courage is not the absence of fear. Demonstrating courage means doing what is right regardless of the fear of danger, criticism, personal hardship, or popular opinion. Demonstrating courage includes confronting and attempting to correct injustice and unfairness.

> *The ultimate measure of a man is not where he stands in moments of comfort and convenience, but where he stands at times of challenges and controversy.*
> - Martin Luther King, Jr.

Courage is having the strength to maintain one's values in the face of opposition, being willing to face and overcome pain and pressure. You gain confidence and strength by facing up to fear and overcoming it. By so doing, you learn that you can often do that which you thought you couldn't.

15. **Love** – Understand that love is, foremost, a verb. Love is something you do. Love is demonstrated by the sacrifices you make for others. Do love.

    Love as a feeling is okay. Love your family and friends. Love your country, love nature, love the less fortunate. Give to what you love. It helps the objects of your love prosper and thrive, and you to grow. Loving others can bring great joy. Remember that both kinds of love require that you first love yourself, in spite of your flaws.

    Being a person of strong character means understanding what to do, being willing to do it, and then actually doing it. It means having the integrity to refuse to do what is wrong and having the courage to do what is right. Courage is not just facing danger. It takes moral courage to refuse to go along with others who are doing something wrong, and to tell the truth when a lie would be more self-serving.

    These values and principles that make up character are guidelines for human conduct that have been proven to have enduring, intrinsic value. Integrating them into your character will make your life richer, more effective and more satisfying. Practice them, make them habits, and pass them on. Of all the variables that determine how you live your life, character matters most. Character is the bedrock that enables you to deal effectively with the circumstances and challenges of life. Mold it well and it will serve you well.

C. How to Mold Your Character

Developing a strong, virtuous character does not happen by wishing it were so. You have to work at it. Character is about more than doing good. It means being good. The following are practices that help build a virtuous character. The details of "how to" are addressed in Part V - Strategies for Taking Control of Your Future.

1. Practice the Golden Rule – Do unto others as you would have them do unto you.
2. Choose values and principles wisely and then live them.
3. Learn from every experience. No matter how good or bad, every experience has something to teach you. View failures as opportunities to learn. Think about it.
4. Associate with people of virtuous character, people you respect. Character is contagious.
5. Take responsibility for your actions. Keep promises. Meet commitments.
6. Develop a purpose and mission statement for your life.
7. Set ambitious goals and develop plans to meet them.
8. Commit to building your character. Develop a self-improvement plan. Strive, each day, to become a better you.
9. Practice resilience. Believe that you can bounce back from setbacks. Keep getting up when knocked down.

10. Exercise self-control. Rationally choose your actions and reactions. Don't let negative emotions determine your responses.
11. Practice empathy and compassion. Strive to understand the feelings of persons who are hurting and find ways to help.
12. Be inclusive. Respect and celebrate human differences.
13. Engage with someone who is "different" from you, someone of a different culture. Listen, learn, share. Everyone has something to teach and something to learn.
14. Lose or win graciously. Win or lose, be a good person.
15. Work willingly. The easy way is not always the best way.
16. Be kind, even when circumstances and provocations tempt you to act unkindly.
17. Develop meaningful relationships. Be the kind of friend you would like to have.
18. Be persistent/tenacious. If something doesn't work, try an alternative.
19. Find and practice ways to serve others.
20. Celebrate and preserve the beauty of the earth and all nature.
21. Learn to learn. Life is a school, complete with tests. The tests can help us learn. Life will be more interesting and exciting if you are constantly learning.
22. Read. The more you read, the more you will know.
23. Learn to listen, really listen. Listening is the most essential skill to learn for dealing effectively with people. It takes intention, concentration and effort.
24. Learn to use time wisely. It is the most precious resource we have.
25. Develop wisdom. Wisdom develops out of intellectual virtues, but is based on knowing how to behave in the absence of perfect knowledge. Real wisdom requires the balancing of head and heart.

Building character is not about being better than others, but becoming better than you used to be. Character is built in the process of resolving your inner confrontation between right and wrong. It is about being strong in times of temptation, dependable in times of testing, having a worthy purpose, and having the courage to do what is right.

Don't expect to be perfect. No one is. Learn from your mistakes and attempt to be better. Stay true to your convictions about fundamental values and truths.

Character counts! Consider carefully the traits you wish to build into your character, and regularly assess your progress. Listing those traits on the worksheet in Appendix F will help you think through this important element for taking control of your future, and provide a useful checklist for determining progress.

Case Study 4, at the end of this chapter, is the story of a couple who demonstrated worthy values and principles, and strong characters. They overcame significant adversities to live admirable lives. Please read and reflect on what enabled their achievements.

CASE STUDY 1 - LEARNING FROM BAD EXPERIENCES

My name is Chuck.

One evening my dad came into my room. With tears in his eyes, he told me that the doctors said my cancer had returned. I was dumbstruck. I was 14 years old. My immediate concern was what this meant for the upcoming school trip to Washington, DC. I had been looking forward to the trip and really wanted to go.

It took a while for the reality to sink in. I had my first bout with the disease when I was three. I had surgery for liver cancer. I didn't remember much about it. This time the cancer was in my colon. The doctor recommended immediate surgery. I pleaded with him to postpone the surgery until after the class trip. He reluctantly agreed.

I made the trip and had a great time with my friends. I was able to put the diagnosis out of my mind for a while.

Up to this time my life had been pretty routine. I had recovered from the first illness and had been healthy. Schoolwork and swim practice, which had previously seemed like chores, I now realized were blessings. I wondered what lay ahead. I thought I would spend a week in the hospital and then hit the weights to get back in shape for swimming. Instead, I spent the next several weeks in and out of the hospital.

When I awoke after the surgery, the pain was so severe, I wanted to die. Recovery took longer than I anticipated. During my hospital stay, I gained a whole new perspective about my life. I got to know some of the other young people in the hospital, and realized that many of them were worse off than I. For some of them, it was a struggle just to hang on to a thread of hope. I recovered and eventually went home. Some of the others were not so fortunate. They never got to return home.

I came out of the hospital a different person. I'm thankful that I'm alive and have the opportunity to make choices that shape my life. Fighting cancer taught me many valuable lessons. This may sound strange but, it turned out to be a blessing, for it made me a much stronger and determined person, and helped me appreciate the blessings I enjoy. Some of the kids I met would have been so thrilled to be able to go to school and live a normal life, simple things that we take for granted. This realization had a major impact on me. Health is never certain. Any day could be your last. I'm thankful I get to make choices about how I am going to react to each situation. I ask myself daily if I am living my life in a positive and fulfilling way. I try to live every day to its fullest. Life is a gift.

Chuck returned to school and competitive swimming. He went to college, qualified for the varsity swim team, and set several school records.

What did Chuck learn from his experience in the hospital?

What values did he demonstrate?

What principles did he employ?

How would you describe his character?

CASE STUDY 2 - A CALCULUS PUZZLE

Jill Brown is a freshman at Beckman College. She is a music major and is doing well in all her courses except calculus, which has been a struggle for her. She is preparing for the first semester final exam and is worried about passing.

Fortunately, the exam is a take-home test she can complete when and where she chooses.

The night before the exam must be turned in, she is in the campus library, which is open 24 hours a day during exam week. She intends to pull an "all-nighter," if necessary, to complete the test.

When she takes a break to go to the vending area, she overhears two students from her calculus class talking about the exam. Alan and Scott are discussing problem number five, which Jill had read over and found especially difficult to understand. They are also comparing calculations and notes.

Beckman College has a strict honor code. It specifically addresses take-home exams and specifies that upon submitting such an exam the student must sign a statement indicating: "Neither I nor anyone that I know of has received or given help to another taking this exam."

Jill takes the honor code seriously. She realizes that the code makes take-home exams possible and that she would have a hard time passing the exam if it were not of that type.

Jill concludes that Scott and Alan are violating the code and the code requires that she disclose their actions. She is in a quandary about what to do. They have seen her and she is unsure about how they will react. She does not want to be a "snitch," but feels like she has some obligation. She decides that if she explains the situation to them they may stop.

She tells them she couldn't help overhearing them discussing the exam and wanted to remind them that we have to sign a pledge that we neither received help, nor gave help to anyone else taking the exam.

Scott and Alan scoff and say that they know all about the honor code and what they are doing is not a violation. Alan says that Scott did not understand one of the questions and he was simply explaining the question to him. He said "That's not cheating, only helping."

Scott pointed out that during freshman orientation they signed a pledge to honor all others by building relationships of support, respect, and trust. "That's all we were doing. That's an important part of the honor code."

Is Jill obligated to report what she observed in the library to the calculus professor?

Is she lying if she signs the pledge without reporting what she observed?

What would you do if you were Jill?

CASE STUDY 3 - IN WANT OF A SIGNATURE

Jim Johnson is a sophomore at Shamrock High. He is new to the school because his father was recently transferred to the city by his company.

When Jim's math teacher, Ms. Miller caught two of his classmates copying Jim's answers to a quiz. She gave him a note, with instructions to take it to his father, get his father's signature, and return it to her tomorrow.

Jim was not comfortable allowing his new friends to copy his work, but he was trying to fit in and didn't know how to say no. He is short on self-confidence and anxious about developing friends in his new school.

He had tried out for the school football team, but was cut after the first week of practice. He is planning to try out for the soccer team, in the hope of making new friends.

Jim's father is a strict disciplinarian and always holds Jim accountable for his actions, especially since Jim's mother died. Jim is almost certain that his father would be upset by the note and likely prohibit him from trying out for the soccer team. Jim is also afraid that his father will contact Ms. Miller and/or the parents of the other students involved and cause him further embarrassment.

Jim is thinking that it is unfair if he is punished for something from which he did not benefit. After all, he was not cheating, he was merely trying to help his new friends. It was not his fault that his friends chose to cheat.

As he is staring at the note, he is thinking that he could forge his father's signature, or have one of his friends forge it. Ms. Miller would never know, since she has never seen his father's signature. He had seen that work for one of his friends at his previous school.

If you were in Jim's situation, would you forge your father's signature?

What would you do?

If you were a friend of Jim's and he asked you to forge his father's signature, what would you do?

What are the values and principles involved here?

What would you have done if it were your friends who asked for your answers to the quiz?

CASE STUDY 4 - THE NELSON AND MARIA GANT STORY

I researched the lives of, and wrote a book about, Nelson and Maria Gant, former slaves who became prosperous and respected citizens of a community in Ohio. Their story illustrates the importance and power of values, principles, and character. (The book is entitled: *Nelson T. Gant – From Slave to Prosperous Business Owner and Respected Citizen*)

Synopsis Of The Gant Story

Lives as Slaves

Nelson T. Gant was an African American slave, born in 1821, on a tobacco plantation in Virginia. His life was marked by drama, from the very beginning. His mother died giving birth to him. He was "adopted" and reared by another female slave on the same plantation, whose name he took as his own. Nelson was documented as a mulatto, (half African American and half white). Anna Maria was a "house" slave, to a different owner, in a nearby town.

Because he was intelligent, courteous, conscientious, and a diligent worker, Nelson, while in his teens, was selected to be the personal manservant, or valet, to the owner of the plantation. As such, he labored in the "big house", rather than in the fields.

Nelson and Maria met, fell in love, and were married. The ceremony was conducted, in 1843, by an ordained minister in the home of Maria's owner. Although married, the couple could not live together. They continued to reside in the homes of their respective owners and to carry on their duties as slaves.

Challenges in Virginia

Nelson was made a free man by the last will and testament of his owner, who died in 1845. Nelson was free, but Maria was still a slave. Nelson appealed to Maria's mistress to free her, saying he could not live without his beloved. Her mistress refused.

Nelson resolved that he would purchase Maria's freedom. He entered into a contract to fell trees and cut 500 cords of wood at 40 cents per cord. It took him nearly nine months to fulfill the contract. He offered the money he had saved to Maria's mistress. She laughed at him and again refused to release Maria.

Nelson left, promising Maria that he would return for her.

He traveled to the Zanesville, Ohio area, where the other slaves from the plantation where he grew up had relocated. There he met some abolitionists, who loaned him money to attempt to buy Maria's freedom.

He returned to Virginia and offered the borrowed funds to Maria's mistress. She scoffed at him and again refused.

Nelson and Maria, in desperation, decided she would run away.

The following excerpt from the book indicates what happened next:

> *They met outside Leesburg and headed to Washington, D. C. They walked the approximately 40 miles. Gant related that he carried Maria on his back a good part of the way.*
>
> *Nelson had been referred, to the address of someone in the Underground Railroad, who, he was told, would help them.*

They reached the address, tired and hungry. A man met them at the door with tears in his eyes. He told them he had been arrested and was under constant surveillance for helping another runaway slave. He pleaded with them to go away before they got him into trouble. He gave them the name and address of an African–American man who would help them.

Betrayal

They went to the address of the second man and were received cordially. But instead of shelter, they found betrayal. They were exhausted and starving, having been afraid to stop on the way to seek food for fear of being apprehended. They gave this man some money to go buy them food. He left, supposedly to buy food, but returned with six policemen. Nelson and Maria were arrested. Nelson was determined to resist, but Maria dissuaded him and they were taken to jail.

Nelson and Maria spent 13 days in a Washington D.C. jail. Through the efforts of Maria's mistress, the governor of Virginia had them extradited back to Leesburg for trial. Nelson was bound and thrown on top of a stagecoach for transport to Leesburg.

Maria spent 22 days in the Leesburg jail. While in jail, she was threatened with being turned over to a slave broker and "sold south," if she declined to testify that Nelson had convinced her to run away. She stuck to her story that she ran away on her own and Nelson followed her.

Nelson was charged with "stealing" a slave, a serious crime in Virginia. He spent weeks in jail, which he described as a loathsome place, awaiting trial. During his wait, he was informed by his attorney that he would likely be convicted. He was nearly overcome by despair. Then something happened that improved his prospects:

> *Then God raised me up a true friend in my trouble. Thomas Nichols, a worthy Quaker, for whom I had once done some insignificant service, came into the jail one day and handed to me through the bars a roll of money, saying he could not sleep while I lay there; that if I got out, I was honest, and would repay him, and that if not, he could well spare the money.*

Nichols also convinced a well-known Quaker lawyer to defend Nelson at his trial.

Nelson's trial was held in December of 1846. Through the eloquent efforts of his attorney, Nelson was acquitted. He was free again, but Maria was still a slave.

After the trial, some local businessmen convinced Maria's mistress that she should sell Maria to Nelson. She finally agreed. Nelson borrowed more money, from the cousin of his lawyer, and Maria received her freedom papers in February of 1847.

Paying Debts

Maria and Nelson were free, but encumbered with huge debts. They decided to stay in Virginia to pay them off. The two lived with and worked for Nichols and his wife for several months, to repay the money Nichols had loaned them. Then they lived and worked, for over two years, at a boarding school for girls, owned by the cousin of Nelson's attorney, who had also loaned them money. During that time their first daughter was born.

Nelson's legal problems were not over. Virginia law stipulated that if a freed slave stayed in Virginia for more than 12 months after being freed, he would be apprehended, sold at auction, and returned to slavery. While working to repay the money loaned to him for the purchase of Maria's freedom, Nelson was indicted on those charges. His trial was postponed several times and the charges were eventually dropped in July of 1850.

Shortly thereafter, Maria, Nelson, and their daughter left Virginia for Ohio.

Life in Ohio

With the assistance of one of the abolitionists he had met on his earlier visit, Nelson went to work for a grower and marketer of farm produce.

Nelson worked hard and was frugal with his money. This former slave, who until age 24 was considered "property", became a property <u>owner</u> for the first time in March of 1853, two and a half years after arriving in Ohio with 50 cents in his pocket. While still employed, he purchased 32 acres of land for $1,287 and began raising crops to sell for his own account. After his employer died in 1855, Nelson became fully self-employed, as a supplier of produce.

The constitution of the state of Ohio prohibited slavery, but it would be naïve to think the Gants' experience with prejudice ended with their move to a free state. Zanesville had a market house, or "farmer's market," where local producers sold their goods directly to consumers. When Nelson attempted to obtain a space in that marketplace, he ran into serious resistance from the white stall owners. In time he won them over and purchased a stall. A "colored newspaper" recounted the events:

> *Everything was closed to Gant, on account of color. His indomitable will and persistence began to open the way. He purchased a small farm and began its work. Mob violence was threatened him if he attempted to purchase a stall at the market house. His determination soon quieted the mob and the stall was purchased.*

Nelson became adept at buying and selling land. At one point he purchased 250 acres for $10,500 and "flipped" it two months later for $15,000. When he died in 1905, he owned over 300 acres of land.

He was an astute business man. On one of the parcels of land he purchased, he developed a coal mine, which became a major supplier to the local market and contributed significantly to his wealth. He also owned a salt lick, and sold block ice, cut from a nearby river.

Gant was frequently referred to as a millionaire. In 1905, his estate was valued at a little over $100,000, a long way from a million, but a lot of money in 1905. It represented a significant accomplishment for someone who started as an orphan slave.

Maria was no mere adornment. She was Nelson's rock, his accomplice. She bore his children, was a loving mother and an able manager of the household. Nelson credited her with bringing him to God. She was a person of admirable character. Maria died in 1877. Bishop Daniel Payne wrote the following in her obituary:

> *She was equally diligent in her visitations to the sick, and ready to relieve the wants of the poor without respect of race or color. A remarkable instance of this character was revealed soon after her death, in the testimony of an Irish woman who went to Mr. Gant to inquire if the report of his wife's death was true. Having been informed of its certainty,*

she broke into bitter lamentations, saying, "O that good woman is gone! She's gone! She's gone! When I was in need of some money to buy me a cow, that I might have wherewithal to get food for my children, I went from house to house to borrow what I needed, but no one would loan me; then I came to Mrs. Gant; I told her my wants, she took out her purse and, putting 19 dollars in gold in my hands, said she 'take this money and if you ever be able, pay me back; if not then, I give it freely to you.'"

Contributions to Church and Community

The Gants became highly respected citizens of Muskingum County and their adopted state of Ohio. They served their community well. Nelson was one of the founders and a trustee of Zanesville's first community hospital, and also a trustee of Woodlawn Cemetery.

Nelson was a trustee and steward of the African Methodist Episcopal (A.M.E.) Church. When that church conducted a campaign to construct a new building, the Gants contributed $5,000 of the $7,000 total cost.

Nelson was also elected to the Board of Trustees for the denomination.

Nelson served on the Board of Trustees of Wilberforce University. His association with the A.M.E. Church put him in contact with Daniel Payne, who was president of that university. Both Nelson and Payne were delegates to the first worldwide conference of the denomination held in London in 1881.

Nelson and Politics

Nelson was active in politics as a member of the Republican Party. An 1890 article in a Columbus, Ohio newspaper indicated that Congressman Van Voorhis of the fifth district depended on Nelson to reach all his people in Zanesville politics.

In 1897, Nelson received a letter from an African American political group, asking for his support in defeating the governor in the upcoming election. He adamantly declined in a letter stating the reasons for his loyalty to the governor. The appeal and Nelson's response were published in several newspapers around the state.

Ohio Governor Bushnell appointed Nelson Gant as one of the delegates to represent Ohio at the Tennessee Centennial and International Exposition at Nashville in 1897, (an early version of subsequent "World Fairs").

Nelson and the Underground Railroad.

Nelson was active in abolitionist activities. A brochure for the Putnam Underground Railroad Interpretive Center in Zanesville states that: "UGRR operatives Nelson T. Gant and Joshua M. Simpson were leaders from an extremely active African American population."

Nelson was reputed to have fed and sheltered slaves in the basement of his home and to transport them to other "safe houses," while hidden in the false bottoms of his produce wagons. These activities were in violation of the Fugitive Slave laws and were thus conducted at great risk.

The National Park Service's *National Underground Railroad Network to Freedom* recognized the Gant home as an

Underground Railroad site in 2004, and placed a commemorative plaque in the front yard.

The Gant story is an impressive account of an extraordinary couple who, through exhibiting exemplary values, principles, and character, overcame multiple adversities to build lives of honor and respect. There is much to the story from which we all can learn.

Life Lessons from the Gant Story

Nelson and Maria demonstrated sound values and strong traits of character that we would do well to emulate. The story should in no way be interpreted as indicating that character alone can overcome the evils of slavery. Nelson and Maria's lives would have been significantly different had Nelson not been freed in his owner's will. Once freed, their values and characters enabled them to excel.

In the following references to their story, identify and write in the values and character traits demonstrated.

1. When his initial attempt to persuade Maria's owner to free her failed, Nelson worked for months to earn money to buy her freedom.

    Values: _____

    Character Trait(s):_____

2. When his initial attempt to buy Maria's freedom failed, Nelson borrowed money in Ohio and returned to try again.

Values: _____

Character Trait(s): _____

3. When his second attempt to purchase Maria's freedom failed, they decided to flee.

   Values: _____

   Character Trait(s): _____

4. Even when faced with the threat of being sold to a plantation further south, Maria refused to testify against Nelson.

   Values: _____

   Character Trait(s): _____

5. After borrowing more money in Virginia to purchase Maria's freedom, the Gants stayed in Virginia, at the risk of their freedom, to work off their debts there.

   Values: _____

   Character Trait(s): _____

6. Nelson and Maria worked hard and saved money to buy land.

   Values: _____

   Character Trait(s): _____

7. Nelson became a very successful businessman.

   Values: _____

   Character Trait(s): _____

8. Nelson and Maria were very supportive, both monetarily and through participation, to church and community.

   Values: _____

   Character Trait(s): _____

9. Maria loaned/gave money to a poor white widow to buy a cow so she could provide milk for her children.

   Values: _____

   Character Trait(s): _____

10. At great personal risk, Nelson helped runaway slaves as an active participant in the Underground Railroad.

    Values: _____

    Character Trait(s): _____

11. Nelson became very involved in politics.

    Values: _____

    Character Trait(s) _____

12. Nelson and Maria ensured that their children had the benefits of music lessons and college educations. Nelson served as a university trustee.

   Values: _____

   Character Trait(s) _____

Mold Your Character

The Nelson and Maria story vividly demonstrates that, while you cannot always control circumstances, molding your character with proven values and principles enables you to deal more effectively with what life brings.

PART II - SOME DECISIONS SHAPE YOUR LIFE

Values, principles and character define who you are. Personal choices determine the quality of your life, and obviously, some choices have a greater impact than others. In this section we will look at two of the most critical areas of choice: how you handle relationships with people in your life, and some things you should exclude from your life.

CHAPTER 4 - NURTURE PERSONAL RELATIONSHIPS

Friendships and personal relationships are critical determinants of the satisfaction and meaning in life. Choose your friends well. Choose those who share your values and principles. To the extent possible, choose your associates well. Then respect and nurture your relationships.

Harvard Medical School conducted a decades long study of factors that contributed to a life considered well lived. Dr. George Vaillant, a psychiatrist and professor, followed the results of the study for over 20 years. He was quoted as saying: "the studies show the only thing that really matters in life are your relationships to other people."

> **Value and Respect Relationships**
>
> My sister hates it when I invade her privacy. I know this because I read it in her diary.

The study confirmed that, when assessing the "success" of their lives, the participants rated connectedness: to family, friends, neighbors and co-workers, as the most important contributor.

To develop effective relationships, you must understand what motivates people, what they value most in their lives, and what fears, biases, prejudices, and aspirations determine the choices they make. According to Phillip McGraw, Ph.D., who rose to fame on Oprah Winfrey's show, the number one fear among all people is rejection.

The number one need is acceptance, and everyone approaches every situation with a least some concern for "what's in it for me?" Realizing what characteristics make people "tick" helps you build relationships that work.

Relationships Matter! They enrich our lives. Your relationships are critical to your well-being and effectiveness. How then should you treat your relationships?

A. Practice The Golden Rule!

Do unto others as you would have them do unto you.

This simple, yet immensely powerful, concept has the potential to change lives (especially yours) and to change the world.

Think about how different the world would be if we would all just follow this basic guideline for respecting the value of other lives. There would be no war, no crime, no hatred, no class conflict, no social strife. In this simple concept, humankind has literally had for centuries the answer to most of the world's problems, but refuses to recognize and implement that answer.

Many of us acknowledge the wisdom of the message, but fail to follow it for a variety of reasons. Instead, we are focused on "me" and what's in it for "me". We are distrustful and fearful of those with different skin colors, religions, social class, language, etc. It also violates our sense of what is "fair" – "people treat me poorly, why should I be nice to them?" etc. etc. These excuses take many forms, but none are legitimate reasons for not doing what is admittedly hard work, but the right thing to do.

This is not a new concept, nor, as many of us Christians like to believe, is it unique to Christianity. We associate it with Jesus's Sermon on the Mount, when in fact the concept was recognized as foundational and critical to human relationships by many cultures hundreds of years before Jesus preached its value. I was interested to find the following examples:

- *In everything, do to others what you would have them do to you.*
  Matthew 7:12, Luke,6:31

- *You shall love your neighbor as yourself.*
  Matthew 22:40

- *Hurt not others with that which pains yourself*
  – Buddhism

- *Do not impose on others what you yourself do not desire.*
  – Confucius

- *This is the sum of duty: do naught to others which if done to thee would cause thee pain.* - Hinduism

- *No one of you is a believer until he desires for his brother that which he desires for himself.* – Islam

- *What is hateful to you, do not do to your neighbor.*
  – Judaism/Talmud

- *Whatever is disagreeable to yourself do not do unto others.*
  – Zoroastrianism

- *Chose thou for thy neighbor that which thou chooseth for thyself.* - Baha'

- *One who is going to take a pointed stick to pinch a baby bird should first try it on himself to feel how it hurts.*
  - Nigerian Proverb

- *A man should wander about treating all creatures as he himself would be treated.* - Jainism

I particularly like the Nigerian version. Note that the Jainism version extends the courtesy to all "creatures."

People tend to treat you as you treat them. The more you demonstrate respect for others, the more likely it is that they will show respect to you. Paying attention to and working at building positive relationships will result in a network of strong connections.

If we would but follow the Golden Rule we would feel good about ourselves and make the world a better place, because of our contributions. The Golden Rule has "Golden Possibilities." **PRACTICE IT.** Vow every morning that today you will treat others as you would like to be treated, regardless of how they treat you. Your life will be richer and far less stressful.

B. Value Family

Ties to family are extremely important. It is from family that a child forms values, develops a sense of safety and belonging, develops aspirations, learns to love, and to manage human relationships. It is from what a child learns in family that communities, societies, nations and the world are formed.

Children learn from instruction, but they learn more indelibly from example. They model what they see demonstrated by parents, siblings and others of influence. As adults, we typically significantly underestimate this effect. Children will do what we do, much more readily than doing what we say. This places a huge responsibility on parents, older siblings, and adults to be appropriate role models.

What do most people say on their deathbeds? They don't say "I wish I had made more money". What they say is: "I wish I had spent more time with my family."
— David Rubenstein

Value family, make family a priority, always be there for family, provide support when needed, be loyal to family, enjoy family, create and nurture family traditions and strengthen and nurture family relationships.

The only things that are really permanent are love, family and friendship. At the end of the day, that's what it really boils down to. The rest is just stuff. — Jared Kushner.

C. Nurture a Few Close Friends

Friendship is a very special kind of relationship. We all need friends. Numerous studies show that there is a direct relationship between happiness and the breadth and depth of one's friendships. A friend is someone who can sense what a friend needs and is ever willing to help meet that need. Making friends and keeping friends is not always easy. The way to <u>have</u> the kinds of friends you want and need, is to <u>be</u> the kind of friend you want to have. The following are some tips for being a good friend:

- Be a good listener and don't try to dominate conversations. People often need to "unload," to air their concerns and problems. Having someone they can trust to share their burdens is a real asset.
- Never attempt to persuade friends to do something that is inconsistent with their values or ethics.
- Take the initiative. Demonstrate that you wish to be friendly. People often confuse reticence with arrogance.
- Demonstrate real interest in your friends' lives and what interests them.

- Be slow to judge. Be willing to get to know a person's true character.
- Be willing to forgive small mistakes. Don't expect friends to be perfect, but set limits.
- Be loyal to friends. Don't criticize them behind their backs or break confidences. Defend them without being untruthful.
- Act like you want your friends to act.
- Keep promises.
- Perform small acts of kindness.
- When you make a mistake, say "I'm sorry."
- Compassionately help friends with shortcomings, but don't become a critic. Criticism destroys friendships.
- Encourage friends to be their best and support their positive efforts.

When choosing friends (it *is* your choice), consider the above as criteria. Choose wisely, because one tends to become like those with whom one associates. While true friends are important, don't become friend dependent. Friends are human and imperfect. Don't let them control who you are. Choose friends based on character, not wealth, social status, or popularity.

Choose friends, not for what they can do for you, but for the blessing of the relationship.

The test of true friendship is whether or not you are a better person when you are with the friend. Choose well. When you have a true friend, let that friend know how important you consider the friendship to be.

D. Recognize That We Are All Related

Relationships with those outside immediate family and friends are important as well. There is an increasing awareness in some circles that we are all related, and that this has significant implications.

The Indigenous People of this country seemed to have grasped this concept.

One of the more unique aspects of traditional Native American culture is the depth of understanding and appreciation of the interconnectedness and interdependence of all people and all things. This concept was often expressed with the phrase: "we are all related." In the Sioux culture, prayers were often concluded with the phrase "for all my relations," the meaning of which included: family, tribe, all the nations of two leggeds in the world, the four leggeds, the winged creatures and all the earth's living things.

Native Americans were not the first to understand this truth. In the sixth century BCE, the Buddha said:

The practice of making others happy is based upon the clear understanding of life, which is Oneness. In deep gratitude, let us realize this Oneness of all life, the heart of which is compassion.

In the first century, the Stoic philosopher Seneca wrote:

All that you behold, that which comprises both god and man, is one – we are the parts of one great body.

This concept, that every living thing within the universe is related, has moral implications. It means that we each have a responsibility to care for all living things, for maintaining balance and harmony in the world, and demonstrating respect for all things that live. Because we are all related, we should strive to live in harmony with all people and all living things.

In the book *GROUNDED,* published in 2015, Diana Butler Bass uses these words to explain the 'big bang' theory of creation:

> *The big bang's simplest insight, and the one with the most profound implications for understanding God and contemporary spirituality, is straightforward: everything that exists was created at the same time; thus all things are connected by virtue of being made of the same matter. This dust (matter) has, throughout time, formed and reformed into gases, worlds and living beings… According to this scientific theory, everything is connected with everything else. Quite literally, Human Beings, (and everything else) are made of stardust.*

In her book *THE SACRED DEPTHS OF NATURE,* Ursula Goodenough, one of America's premier biologists, states the following:

> *So, all the creatures on the planet today share a huge number of genetic ideas. Most of my genes are like most gorilla genes, but they're also like many of the genes in a mushroom. I have more genes than a mushroom, to be sure, and some critical genes are certainly different, but the important piece to take in here is our deep interrelatedness, our deep genetic homology, with the rest of the living world.*

Scientists are not the only group of moderns who have embraced this concept of interrelatedness. In a book titled *PROCESS THEOLOGY,* Bruce G. Epperly lists the following among what he labels as the "Essential Concepts of Process Theology:"

- *All living things exist in relationship with one another. We live in an interdependent universe in which each moment of experience arises from its environment, whose influence provides both limits and possibilities.*
- *Experience is universal, though variable, and extends beyond humankind. While creatures differ in complexity*

and impact on the world, every creature has some minimal level of responsiveness to its environment.
- *The universality of experience leads to the recognition that every creature is inherently valuable and deserves moral consideration.*
- *Process Theology values all creation, even apart from its impact on human life... flora and fauna are valuable not just because we appreciate their beauty but because they experience some level of joy and sorrow. They matter to God and, accordingly, should enter into our own moral calculations.*

In his book, *ETERNAL LIFE: A NEW VISION,* John Shelby Spong wrote:

In fact we now know that all matter within our universe, from the farthest star to the content of your body and mine is interconnected. Such a sense of interdependency has, before our time, never even been imagined. Human life is kin not just to the great apes but to the cabbages and indeed even to the plankton in the sea... That insight leads to the conclusion that while separation may have been our perception, it is not the law of the universe. A deep interrelated unity is.

Despite their differences in perspective, scientists and theologians are reaching the same conclusions as did the Indigenous People of this continent - every living thing is interconnected and interdependent - **We Are All Related.**

Our world would be an immeasurably better place, a place of balance, harmony and peace, if we could learn to treat all humans as brothers and sisters and all living things as sacred, and thus worthy of respect.

E. Apply Proven Relationship Principles

There are principles that have been proven effective for making relationships work, within and outside the family.

1. Earn Trust - Trust is the foundation of all effective relationships. In *The Speed of Trust*, Stephen Covey wrote:

   There is one thing that is common to every individual, relationship, team, family, organization, nation, economy, and civilization throughout the world - one thing which, if removed, will destroy the most powerful government, the most successful business, the most thriving economy, the most influential leadership, the greatest friendship, the strongest character, the deepest love. On the other hand, if developed and leveraged, that one thing has the potential to create unparalleled success and prosperity in every dimension of life. Yet, it is the least understood, most neglected, and most underestimated possibility of our time. That one thing is trust.

Trust is built on integrity and competence. Trust must be earned. We earn trust by meeting commitments, by telling the truth, and doing what we say we are going to do. Being trustworthy means that those with whom we interact are confident of our motives, our ethics, our reliability, and our abilities.

Trust is crucial. EARN IT!

Please read and reflect on the story in Case Study 5, "Glendale Grass," at the end of this chapter.

2. Be Real – To develop meaningful relationships requires that we be real, that we drop pretenses and reveal our true feelings and our true selves. Being authentic means admitting that you

are a work in progress and are not perfect. It means being genuinely empathetic.

A key lesson in life is to understand our real selves, to be real in our relationships and to see the authenticity in others.

Please read and think about the story in Case Study 6, "Trying to Fit In," at the end of this chapter.

3. Demonstrate Respect - Effective people have well established standards and expectations for personal relationships. Principles for relationships are based upon assumptions of mutual respect. Some of the principles considered necessary for achieving harmonious relationships are as follow:

    - Always tell the truth. Lying destroys relationships
    - Listen carefully.
    - Never interrupt when another is talking.
    - Seek to understand. Visualize yourself in the other person's "shoes."
    - Be honest.
    - Keep commitments.
    - Accept responsibility for your words and actions.

4. Think Win/Win - Many significant decisions involve interactions with others. Author Stephen Covey contends that to make these decisions effective, they should be constructed as "Win/Win":

    Win/Win is a frame of mind and heart that constantly seeks mutual benefit in human interactions. Win/Win means that agreements or solutions are mutually beneficial, mutually satisfying. With Win/Win solutions, all parties feel good about the decision and feel committed to the action plan.

Covey continues:

> *Win/Win is based on the paradigm that there is plenty for everybody, that one person's success is not achieved at the expense of, or exclusion of, the success of others. Win/Win is a belief in the Third Alternative. It's not your way or my way; it's a better way, a higher way.*

Each of us is the common denominator in all of our relationships. The attitude that we bring to the relationship determines the quality thereof. Every relationship, no matter how brief, is potentially important because it may alter someone's life.

5. Practice Compassion - Demonstrating compassion, the sharing of someone's pain, discomfort, dilemma, loss, or unfortunate circumstance, is the "right" thing to do. To care enough to take on some of the burden, so that another person does not have to bear problems alone, can be extremely helpful and meaningful, to both the recipient and to the giver.

> *To give pleasure to a single heart by a single act is better than a thousand heads bowing in prayer.*
> - Mahatma Gandhi

Understanding and demonstrating compassion may be critical to the very survival of humankind and the world we share with other creatures. The root of the word is the Latin "compati" which means "to suffer with." But the concept involves more than pity. It involves: (1) being aware of the suffering of others, (2) feeling empathy for the one suffering, and (3) taking action to alleviate that suffering.

> *It is one of the most beautiful compensations of this life that no man can sincerely help another without helping himself.*
> - Ralph Waldo Emerson

Demonstrating compassion develops and strengthens relationships.

6. Respect Personal Differences - One of the greatest sources of strife, conflict, suffering and inhumanity in the world, today and historically, is mankind's attitude toward, and reaction to, <u>differences</u> in: race, religion and culture. Unconscionable atrocities have been committed against fellow humans because they looked, thought, believed and/or prayed differently than the perpetrators. An all-too-common reaction to personal differences is: fear, mistrust and misunderstanding.

What we desperately need is an awareness of, an appreciation of, and a commitment to, genuine, inclusive community, with the term community encompassing family, neighborhood, country, and world. We are all in this together, whether we realize it or not. No matter how much we value our independence, we are mutually dependent.

   a. Tolerance or Acceptance

   Intolerance is despicable, but tolerance is insufficient. We need to do more than tolerate those unlike us. The difference between tolerance and acceptance is huge. "I tolerate" means I consider myself superior, but I will allow the existence of others as long as they do not impinge on my own life and way of doing things, or encroach on my value systems. To simply tolerate means to hardly notice that others exist and to have as little as possible to do with them.

   You're not under attack when others gain rights and privileges you've always had.
   - DaShanne Stokes

To accept others is to place yourself on the same level, so as to know the other, to allow the other the same rights that you expect, and to attempt to understand and respect the other, despite any differences. It means respecting another's right to be different and to attempt to learn from understanding the perspectives of others.

Please read and reflect on the story in Case Study 7, "I Just Want to be Me," at the end of this chapter.

> *We need to give each other the space to grow, to be ourselves, to exercise our diversity. We need to give each other space so that we may both give and receive such beautiful things as ideas, openness, dignity, joy, healing, and inclusion.*
> - Max de Pree

b. Embrace and Promote Inclusiveness

When we speak of inclusiveness, we are not talking about uniformity, but about a mindset that values and celebrates differences. Humans desperately need community. A group based on exclusivity is not a community, but a clique. Real communities are inclusive.

"Loving your neighbor as yourself" is a quotation usually associated with Christianity, but the closely related "do unto others as you would have them do unto you" is a basic value common to many cultures. Living these values is a personal responsibility and should be incorporated into all personal and group relationships.

Values are learned, primarily from family and friends. Children are not born with exclusivity, intolerance and bigotry built in. They have to be taught. In the early 1950's, Rogers and Hammerstein expressed this truth in the words of a song in the score of the musical *SOUTH PACIFIC*:

> *They have to be taught before its too late*
> *before they are six or seven or eight*
> *to hate all the people their relatives hate*
> *they've got to be carefully taught.*

We must carefully practice inclusiveness, acceptance and respect for human dignity. As with most values, we most effectively teach these values by example.

Being an inclusive person means:

- Communicating honestly with each other.
- Respecting and celebrating human differences.
- Transcending differences rather than attempting to obliterate them.
- Genuinely demonstrating an interest in the values, beliefs and worldviews of others.
- Showing compassion – the willingness to share the burdens of others.
- Building relationships that go deeper than superficial niceties.
- Committing to: understanding each other, rejoicing together, mourning together and finding delight in each other.

Seek out and learn from those who are "different."

> *The world is getting too small for both an Us and a Them. Us and Them have become codependent, intertwined, fixed to one another. We have no separate fates, but are bound together in one. And our fear of one another is the only thing capable of our undoing.*
> - Sam Killermann

Americans like to think of ours as a "good" nation, that we are champions of doing what is "right." The documented principles upon which this country was founded assert that: "all men are created equal and have unalienable rights to: life, liberty and the pursuit of happiness." Yet we have, in this country, sanctioned, encouraged and justified some of the most horrible examples of man's inhumanity to man in the history of the world.

Slavery was motivated by greed. Some whites grew rich exploiting the "free" labor of blacks.

Native Americans were nearly exterminated, primarily because of the Euro/Americans' greed for their land. We recoil at the notion of, and condemn the horror of, the European holocaust, in which an estimated 6 million Jews were killed by the Nazis. Yet, we gloss over and mostly fail to acknowledge that Euro/Americans exterminated <u>millions</u> of Native Americans for the purpose of seizing the land upon which they depended for their existence. This systematic extermination was accomplished by direct violence (slaughter) and by more subtle means (blankets deliberately contaminated with smallpox viruses were "traded" to Indians, wiping out entire villages).

Both the African and Indian atrocities were justified in the minds of some Euro/Americans, by the notion that the victims were inferior to whites, that black people and red people were somehow sub-human, more akin to wild animals, unworthy of the rights enjoyed by white people.

I point out these examples, not to "bash" the USA, (I consider it the greatest country the world has known), but to point out the terrible consequences generated by feelings of superiority. We need to be aware of these "errors," so we do not continue to make them.

> *Inclusion works to the advantage of everyone. We all have things to learn and we all have something to teach.*
> - Helen Henderson

While not as overt as slavery and extermination, prejudice, discrimination, and bigotry are manifestations of the same superiority beliefs that fueled these injustices. I URGE YOU NOT TO PARTICIPATE!

I encourage you each to find a way that you can promote inclusiveness, community and social justice in your personal life.

> *The way to be successful is to find a way to be inclusive of everybody. It's the difference between an attitude that looks at diversity and assumes you can be successful despite it, versus an attitude that looks at diversity and assumes you can be successful as a result of it.*
> - "Magic" Johnson

Please read and reflect on the story in Case Study 8, "Where Do I Fit?," at the end of this chapter.

7. Be Kind and Generous.

   Generosity is rooted in the belief that we receive many gifts and thus have the obligation and privilege to "give back." Giving to another enhances the development of relationships, and reinforces the perception that a "good" person is one who shares.

   > *There is a wonderful, almost mystical law of nature that says three of the things we want most – happiness, freedom, and peace of mind – are always attained when we give them to others.*   - John Wooden

8. Serve – Determine How You Will "Give Back."

   Life itself is a gift we did nothing to "earn." In addition, no one makes it through life entirely on his or her own merits. We all owe others. Life is a blessing we should acknowledge by contributing to the lives of others. We can take nothing with us from this life, but we can and should leave behind us something worthwhile. Living a meaningful life means making the world a better place because we lived.

   > *Life's most persistent and urgent question is: "What are you doing for others?"*
   > - Dr. Martin Luther King Jr.

   Giving back is a win-win proposition. By serving, we not only improve the lives of others, but also reap personal benefits. A Harvard Business School study confirmed that: "happier people give more and giving makes people happier, such that happiness and giving may operate in a positive feedback loop." Those who receive help are grateful for the help and volunteers learn that helping others makes them feel better. Unlike giving money, giving time, energy, and effort, provides immediate feedback about what your contribution means to those receiving it. Our lives become richer, fuller, and complete through attending to the healing of others.

Giving generates hope. We can each be part of the problem or part of the solution.

Choose to be one of those who hears and answers. We each have something to offer. Giving should not be driven by feelings of guilt or obligation, but by an expression of gratitude for having the ability to give, and by our response to the understanding that we are all interrelated and interdependent.

> *An individual has not started living until he can rise above the narrow confines of his individualistic concerns to the broader concerns of all humanity.*
> — *Dr.* Martin Luther King, Jr.

A defining factor in living a meaningful life is contributing to something above and beyond self. We should consciously choose to invest time where our efforts will yield a return for others. Gifts do not have to be costly. The gift of friendship, or simply one's presence, can make a difference in a life.

When selecting an area in which to give back, it is important to select a cause in which one has an interest and abilities. That makes it more fun. Do something. Make a commitment. It is better if it represents an on-going commitment rather than a one-time shot. Finding a way to help people help themselves can be particularly rewarding.

Appendix G, contains a list of several ways you can give back. It is by no means exhaustive. Try one or more. Think of some others you can add in the spaces. For more ideas, take a look at *www.volunteermatch.org*.

In the final analysis, all we really own is our lives. It is how we use our lives that determine what kind of people we are. As Mother Teresa observed, *We don't have to do great things, only lots of small things with great love.*

It is by serving and giving that we find life. Relationships matter. Develop and nurture them.

CASE STUDY 5 - GLENDALE GRASS

Nancy James was a church youth group leader. When she received a call from the mother of one of the girls in her youth group, she sensed it meant trouble. She had dealt with the girl before.

Mrs. Johnson asked her if she could come right over to her home. Nancy had a previous commitment, but Mrs. Johnson sounded frantic, so she said she would get there as soon as she could. She called her commitment, rescheduled, and drove to the Johnson's.

The Johnsons lived in a nice part of town and the daughter, Katy, went to the best high school. There were two older siblings, both of whom had a history of problems with alcohol and the law. Katy was a beautiful girl and very bright. For the last year or so she had been hanging out with an older age group. She attended the church youth group intermittently.

Nancy had heard from someone in the group that Katy was into drugs. She had offered Katy confidential help but had been rebuffed with "you're just a busy-body and I don't need your help."

Nancy asked the reason for the call. Katy responded: "Mom found some marijuana and some pills in my drawer and freaked out." Mrs. Johnson replied that she had been putting away some clean clothes and saw what she thought were drugs. Katy yelled: "you had absolutely no right to look. I'm entitled to my privacy."

Nancy asked Mrs. Johnson what happened next. She replied: "My first thought was to tell her father, but I was afraid he would lose his temper and beat her. I told her she was grounded for two weeks. She hates to stay home. Katy yelled that if her mother insisted that she stay home, she would just leave and go to California.

Nancy asked to see the bag. Katy replied that they should leave her stuff alone. Her mom retrieved the bag, which contained over a pound of marijuana and several dozen red capsules. Katy exclaimed, "Mom doesn't care if I'm popping dope. She's just concerned with her friends. You know what she said; 'Katy, what will people think if you get arrested for using drugs.'"

How should Nancy advise Katy?

Was Katy's privacy invaded?

How should Nancy advise Mrs. Johnson?

Should Mr. Johnson be involved?

There is not much trust here between mother and daughter. What might each do to improve it?

CASE STUDY 6 - TRYING TO FIT IN

Susan and I became friends the summer before our sophomore year in high school. My freshman year had not been easy. I was plain and awkward. I preferred reading to socializing. My clothes were not trendy. I had no close friends. I mostly kept to myself.

Susan was totally different. She was articulate and social. She knew a lot about popular music. She always looked good. She was an excellent student. She was very popular. Everyone liked her. I was envious.

We took a summer class together and were paired up as a team for a project. She seemed reluctant to work with me at first, but warmed up, and became actually friendly. After the class was over, we continued to hang out for the rest of the summer. We went to the mall, the beach, and to movies. It was great.

I idolized Susan. She was everything I wanted to be. I started to listen to the music she liked, to watch the TV shows she liked. I began wearing the kinds of clothes she wore. I scheduled my classes so I would be in hers. I signed up for an art class, even though I really wanted to try a theater class I had heard about.

When school started in the fall, Susan introduced me to her friends. She was clearly the leader of the group. I followed them around, laughed at their jokes, agreed with their opinions. I very much wanted to fit in. I didn't want them to think I was a nerd, by disagreeing with them.

One Friday, after school, I hurried to a burger joint near school where we hung out. I slipped into a booth and became absorbed in some homework. I didn't notice when Susan and her friends came in and sat in the booth behind me. They didn't see me either.

All of a sudden, I realized they were talking about me.

One girl said, "She's such a loser."

Another joined in, "Susan, she just follows you around, trying to be you. She copies everything you say and do. She doesn't have a personality of her own."

Susan replied, "I know, I wish she would just leave us alone. We were in a summer class together and now she thinks we're best friends. She should get a life."

I was mortified. I didn't realize she thought of me that way. My heart was broken. My hands were shaking, tears flowed. I got up and ran out the door. They saw me and realized I had heard their conversation.

I ran home and told my mom what happened. I cried for hours. Mom held me and told me that I was special, that I should just be me and that people would like me for who I am. I had heard it before, but this time it struck home. I resolved to do just that.

Susan and her friends didn't talk to me after that. After a while that was ok. I made a lot of changes to my life. I started to wear the clothes I liked, listen to the music I liked and read the books I liked. I joined the theater group and won a part in the school play. Through theater, I made several new friends.

I was in every school play for the remainder of high school, had several lead roles, and won some awards. The great friends I made in the theater group are still my friends today. The rest of my high school experience was incredible.

Despite the pain of the experience, it forced me to discover the person I wanted to be. I realized that those girls who made fun of me did me a favor. The things they said about me were true. They made me understand it. I was just following, just trying to fit in. Had they not opened my eyes, I would have missed some of the best times of my life.

What does pretending to be different than you are, in order to fit in, indicate about you?

Is trying to fit in always a bad thing?

What are some useful guidelines for setting limits on what you will do to fit in?

How did mom help?

What should you consider when selecting a group to which you want to belong?

What are some things we can do to turn what appears to be a disaster into something positive?

CASE STUDY 7 - I JUST WANT TO BE ME

My name is Tim. I'm 17 years old, 6'5', and husky. People think I should be an athlete. But I'm no athlete.

I figured out several years ago that I'm gay. Growing up, I didn't enjoy doing the things that most boys did. Guys in my neighborhood would try to get me to play basketball or football. I wasn't very good. They would make fun of me and call me a faggot, because I was clumsy.

The boys in my neighborhood were ball-playing, rough-necked, pot-smoking guys who picked on people to prove to each other that they were tough and manly.

I couldn't understand why they constantly wanted to harass me and fight with me, just because I was different. The names hurt. So what if I'm gay. I just want to be me.

One Halloween night I was on my way to catch a bus to go to a party. I had on a brand-new set of clothes that my mother had just bought for me. A group of the local toughs came by on bikes and tossed a bottle of urine that soaked my clothes. They rode away laughing. One of them yelled: "How do you like that, faggot?" I screamed and cried, because I knew how much my mother had paid for my new outfit. My brothers offered to beat up the boys who soaked me, but I thought it would only make the situation worse. Later, we did fight and my brothers helped me. The fights made me feel better for a while, but I never felt like I belonged. It seemed like the whole world was against me.

There were some people who helped and supported me. My best friend was Donna. She didn't seem to care that I was gay. She praised me for having the courage to come out to my parents and brothers at an early age. She called me "brave."

Another person who helped me survive was my grandmother. She raised me after my parents died. She taught me kindness, courage, patience and the "Golden Rule." She had lived through a lot of hardships; the Depression, two world wars, poverty and segregation. She told me about watching the bodies of two black teenagers being cut down from a tree where they had been lynched. She would tell me that life wasn't as hard today as it used to be.

My grandmother never tried to change me. Instead she encouraged me to do what I thought was right. I was placed in foster care after she got sick. She called me one evening, and said, "I love you dear. Don't let anyone try to change you." She died two weeks later.

Is a person's sexual orientation a "choice"?

Why do you think some people pick on gays and lesbians?

What does abusing someone because they are "different" say about the abuser?

Have you ever witnessed someone being treated poorly because they were "different" in some way?

Has anyone ever stood up for and supported you when you needed it?

Have you ever tried to support someone who was "different" in some way?

CASE STUDY 8 – WHERE DO I FIT?

I've come to believe that being different is a curse. My parents are Chinese and my name is Chin Lee. I grew up in a mostly black neighborhood, so I never fit in, but I didn't initially think much about race. Then in the first grade, boys started calling me "slant eyes," and making fun of me.

Later, even kids I thought were my friends would make fun of my name, the way I talked, and my looks. They would ask me if I wanted egg rolls for lunch, and squinted their eyes at me.

I knew they were only joking around, but it hurt. They could see that it bothered me, because my face would turn red. That made them laugh.

On the way home from school one day, two black kids started to yell names at me and threw rocks. They called me "Egg Roll Lee." One rock hit me on the arm. It hurt. I was too scared to do anything. I ran home.

To my surprise, it was not just white kids who made fun of me, but Black and Hispanic kids as well. Later, I wondered why Black kids would make racist remarks. It seemed that they should know better, that they would understand how much it hurt. They would say crude things to me, and then complain that they were treated unfairly because of the color of their skin.

When people talk about racism, they are usually thinking black and white. Racism is not limited. Being treated as dirt because I was Asian really hurt me.

One time I did react and it only made things worse. I got angry and into a fight with a guy who was making perverted remarks about all Asian girls. I tried to make him believe that I was not afraid of him, but inside I was scared. He backed off and went away, much to my relief.

Even worse than feeling angry is the feeling of being ashamed of who I am. When I was younger, I used to wish I was white and rich. I used to think about changing my name.

Now I'm uncertain about how I should feel. Should I be angry at the people who belittle me? Should I seek revenge? Should I just be sad? I'm confused about everything. I feel lost and alone.

I grew up in America and my parents insisted that we speak English. I can speak very little Chinese. If I went to China, I wouldn't fit in because I don't know the language. I feel like an alien who doesn't fit anywhere.

Do you, or someone you know, feel "cursed," because of the racial or ethnic group to which you, or they, belong?

Why do you think some people look down on people who are different?

Why do you think people who are discriminated against sometimes discriminate against others?

What can you do personally to avoid discriminating against others?

What can you do personally to help eliminate discrimination?

CHAPTER 5 - EXCLUDE SOME THINGS FROM YOUR LIFE

Some of the most important decisions you make about how to live your life are your choices about what you will exclude from your life. **What you <u>don't</u> need in your life are mind and body altering, toxic substances, specifically drugs, alcohol and nicotine.** These substances destroy the lives of more young people than any of the other problems they face. Please don't dismiss this information as just another example of an adult trying to tell you what to do. Get the facts, understand the implications, and think about these issues. Drugs are widely available. You undoubtedly have been, or will be, pressured to "try" them. The choices are yours. The consequences can be devastating.

A. These Substances Kill People

Harmful drugs are chemical substances that change how your mind and body work. Drugs like heroin, meth, and cocaine are so harmful they are illegal. Opioids can be obtained legally by prescription, but abuses are common. Not all harmful drugs are illegal. Alcohol and tobacco, legally available to all adults, are also drugs. They alter the mind and the body, are addictive and, like illegal drugs, they can be deadly.

Data from The Center for Disease Control (CDC) indicates that:

- 107,941 Americans died from drug overdoses in 2022.
- Excessive use of alcohol causes approximately 140,000 deaths in the United States per year.
- Cigarette smoking causes more than 480,000 deaths in the United States each year. Worldwide, tobacco use causes more than 7 million deaths per year. More than 10 times as many US citizens have died prematurely from cigarette

smoking than have died in all the wars fought by the United States. On average, smokers die 10 years earlier than nonsmokers.

- 24,486 Americans died in 2021 from drug poisoning involving the use of cocaine.

Consider the following account from a grieving mom:

> *My beloved daughter, Chelsea Marie, died on May, 3, 2002 at 8:50 a.m. She was two weeks shy of her senior prom, one month shy of her 18th birthday, and seven weeks away from high school graduation. She was my very best friend.*
>
> *She had an argument with her boyfriend and went to talk to a friend, who gave her ecstasy.*
>
> *I got a call from the police that she was in the hospital from a drug overdose. We arrived to find her unconscious and having powerful seizures. It was horrific. They induced a coma to stop the seizures.*
>
> *For a week we prayed, cried, begged and hoped. She had a high fever, was hooked up to a machine, was breathing through a respirator. My little girl was losing the battle. Her lungs, her brain, her kidneys, her bowels, everything was slowly deteriorating. She was in a vegetative state. She never came out of the coma. Her internal organs stopped functioning, one by one.*
>
> *Me, her dad, her brother, will never be the same. My heart was crushed that day.*

Reflect on the fate of two brothers from Indiana:

> *Nick and Jack Savage were born 18 months apart. They were best friends, good students and stellar athletes. Each served as captain of his high school hockey team during his senior year.*
>
> *Both planned to graduate from college. In the summer of 2015, Nick had finished his freshman year at Indiana University and Jack was heading to Ball State University that fall.*
>
> *While attending a graduation party, Nick and Jack consumed a lethal combination of alcohol and the potent painkiller oxycodone. They were both found unresponsive in their home the next day. They both died from accidental overdoses.*
>
> *Neither had a history of drug use.*

According to the Alcohol Control Center, drunk driving is the nation's number one killer of people between the ages of 15 and 24. A driver with a blood alcohol level of .10 is 12 times as likely to have an accident as someone who is sober.

In the United States, one person is killed in a drunk driving crash every 39 minutes.

The rate of suicides is 32 times higher for alcoholics than for non-alcoholics.

Using these substances is like playing Russian roulette with a loaded gun. You <u>may</u> not die from one try, but if you persist, the results can be deadly. The temporary "high" is not worth the risk.

Please read and think about the situation described in Case Study 9, Is the Thrill Worth the Price?, at the end of this chapter.

B. Other Effects of These Substances on Users.

1. Health Impacts

   Even for the users who do not die directly from these substances, the impact on personal health can be horrendous.

   According to the National Institute on Drug Abuse, in addition to the effects on the brain, illicit drugs can cause or worsen: heart disease, lung disease, stroke, liver malfunction, kidney damage, and infectious diseases such as AIDS and hepatitis. Some drugs damage or destroy nerve cells in the brain and the central nervous system.

   Alcohol can cause liver damage, brain damage, and is the fifth leading cause of cancer.

   CDC data indicates that cigarette smoking harms nearly every organ of the body. Some of the CDC data show:

   - Smokers are 25 times as likely to develop lung cancer as non-smokers.
   - Smokers are 2 to 4 times as likely to suffer from heart disease.
   - Smokers are 2 to 4 times as likely to have a stroke.
   - Smoking can cause cancer almost anywhere in the body.
   - The risk of developing diabetes is 30% - 40% higher for smokers than non-smokers.

2. Behavior Modification

All of these drugs alter brain functions and affect behavior. Often in ways that are harmful and foreign to the way you would act if you were in "your right mind."

Drugs and alcohol lead to loss of coordination, slowed reflexes, distorted vision, poor judgment, memory lapses and blackouts. They cause you to do stupid things. They destroy your ability to control how you act and what you do. You cannot consistently make good decisions while under the influence of mind-altering chemicals.

Some have the misconception that smoking marijuana is relatively harmless. Not so. In addition to leading to the step up to other drugs, marijuana use can significantly alter behavior. According to a study titled *Marijuana Alert III: The Devastation of Personality,* smoking marijuana creates "pot personality," the traits of which include: impaired short term memory, emotional flatness, the dropout syndrome, diminished willpower, diminished concentration, diminished attention span, diminished ability to deal with abstract or complex problems, diminished tolerance for frustration, increased confusion in thinking, impaired judgement, and hostility toward authority. Do these sound like characteristics that you want to "try on?"

In addition to the effects on behavior and mental functioning, there is mounting evidence that marijuana use leads to using even more harmful drugs. This is called the "gateway effect." A study published in the International Journal of Drug Policy in 2015 found that 44.7% of cannabis users progressed to other illicit, and even more harmful, drugs.

The craving for harmful substances drives people to do things they would not do, if not for the craving. There is a high correlation between drug abuse and crime. Bureau of Justice statistics indicate that 17% to 18% of federal & state penitentiary prisoners committed the offenses that put them in prison, to enable them to buy drugs, and that 50% had alcohol related problems.

The power to make choices is life's greatest gift. If you become addicted to something, you give up your freedom to choose.

When I was in college, I had a job working for the president of the university. Part of my job was to serve drinks and food to guests he entertained in his home. One evening, after I served a soft drink to a male guest, a lady in his immediate circle asked him about his choice of beverage. I've never forgotten his reply. He said: "When I was in college I played football. I decided not to drink then because I didn't want to impair my performance on the football field. After graduation I discovered that life is a much tougher game than football, and if I wanted to do my best, I better not start drinking."

3. Distorted Self Perception

Drugs and alcohol distort the user's perception of personal capabilities and self-image. Users often think that their mental and physical abilities are enhanced, when in fact they have been impaired. The most common example is not realizing the extent to which driving skills are impaired.

Many young men think that it is masculine and mature to drink or get high, that it makes them more mature, tough, or more attractive to the opposite sex. Young ladies sometimes think it will make them more appealing to young men, if they participate. In fact, it is neither macho nor appealing to become loud, pushy, and obnoxious, to lose control of bodily functions, or to puke up one's guts. All of which are frequent consequences of doing alcohol and other drugs.

4. Addiction

The term addiction comes from a Latin word for "enslaved." Being enslaved is not a good thing. Think seriously about whether you want to be <u>enslaved</u> to drugs, alcohol or nicotine. Use of these substances at an early age often leads to serious problems. One out of fifteen teen drinkers becomes an alcoholic.

According to a Harvard Medical School publication, addiction exerts a long and powerful influence on the brain, that affects a person in three distinct ways:

- Craving for the object of addiction.
- Loss of control over its use.
- Continuing use of the addictive substance despite adverse consequences.

Addiction is a chronic disease that changes both the structure and function of the brain. Think about what your reaction would be if someone walked up to you with a scalpel and said "I want to alter your brain." That is what is happening when someone encourages you to "try" a potentially addictive substance. Studies by the National Institute on Drug Abuse confirm that these chemicals physically change the areas of the brain that are critical for judgment, decision-making, learning, memory, and behavior control.

No one starts out by saying "I want to become an addict", but it is so easy to get caught up in the snare. These chemical substances affect the brain's pleasure, reward, learning, and memory systems, making it easy to transition from the initial euphoria of the experience to becoming addicted to it; from liking it, to wanting it, to "needing" it.

Most addictions have their roots in the "gateway drugs;" alcohol and marijuana. These substances are harmful in themselves and often lead to more dangerous drugs. Studies of the brains of frequent marijuana users indicate that memory, the ability to solve problems, the speed of processing information, and brain development are all impaired. Alcohol goes directly into the bloodstream and brain, altering thinking and body functions. Don't be trapped into rationalizing that I will only "do" the light stuff.

The pressure to "try" addictive substances can be strong. Reasons cited for starting are many:

- I want to belong – peer pressure.
- Everyone else is doing it.
- I just want to have some fun.
- One time won't hurt.
- Life is boring - I want some excitement.
- I'm curious to see what it's like.
- I have so many problems. I need an escape.
- I'm under so much pressure. I need a relief.
- To rebel against authority – "They can't tell me what to do."

None of these reasons are sufficient justification for giving up control of your mind and your life. There are better ways to deal with these issues.

Be particularly cautious of turning to drugs and alcohol as a means of escaping your troubles. When you are lonely and troubled you may be most vulnerable. Don't assume your miseries will go away because you temporarily escape into oblivion. Drugs and alcohol cannot make you more attractive, smarter, or more popular. Getting drunk or stoned will not solve your problems. The consequences only compound your problems.

Don't rationalize with delusions such as: "It will never happen to me." "I'm strong. I can quit whenever I want." "It's my life, I'm not hurting anyone else." **Do not believe it!** These chemicals are stronger than you are, and they change your willpower and your life. Many of the teens struggling through rehabilitation programs or suffering from the effects of these substances will tell you that they thought it couldn't happen to them.

The following are examples of actual comments by young people who lost control:

"Once I started, I had to keep going. I could not control it. I had to have more."

"I might never have recovered from my coma. I later thought, 'Why did I do that?' It wasn't worth it."

"I was picked up for drunk driving. I fell down when the policeman asked me to walk a line. I spent the night in jail in my vomit-drenched clothes. My mom cried when she picked me up."

"Once, when our source of pot tried up, we switched to beer. It didn't make me feel as good as pot, so I found a new and stronger drug. I was soon hooked. I had to have it."

"To buy the pot and beer I thought I had to have, I started stealing from the homes where I baby sat."

"Once I dried out and returned to somewhat sane behavior, I learned some things about alcohol and that I had a serious problem. For the first time since ninth grade, I felt a yearning to be normal."

Does this sound like a club you want to join? It's your choice.

Once started, quitting is not easy. For example, A National Institute of Drug Abuse survey of adult smokers found that 68% wanted to stop smoking. More than 55% had attempted to quit within the last year. Of those who attempted to quit, only 7.5% succeeded. The developed need for nicotine is strong, just as is the so easily developed need for other drugs.

Treatments for addictions are long, expensive and difficult. It is far better never to start.

C. Effects on Others

Some rationalize that: "It's my life. What I do is nobody else's business." Nothing could be further from the truth. Drug abuse is not just about the abuser. Seeing a life destroyed causes anguish to parents, grandparents, siblings and friends. Younger siblings and friends copy what they see you doing, because they rationalize that if you're doing it, it must be ok. Your altered behavior can impact all those with whom you have contact.

A Point to Ponder: Have you witnessed a friend or acquaintance negatively impacted by drugs and/or alcohol?

Driving under the influence of alcohol or drugs can result in the death or disabling of passengers, and/or total strangers. Aside from the possible penalties involved, think about what it would mean to have such an incident on your conscience for the rest of your life.

On the worksheet in Appendix H, make a list of the names of the persons who would be affected if you were to become addicted to alcohol or other drugs. Think hard about whether you want to do that to them.

D. Dealing with Peer Pressure

If you are like most young people, you dislike rules and attempts to control what you do. Why then, would you be tempted to permit your peers to control you? That's what happens when you give in to peer pressure.

The pressure to go along with the crowd or a "friend," to do something you know you shouldn't do, can be severe. Peer pressure is the number one reason that people start using addictive substances. If you choose not to participate, you will likely be laughed at, dared and ridiculed. Labels like "loser," "nerd," or "chicken," hurt, but giving in means giving up who you want to be, just to be what someone else wants you to be. "Giving in" means giving up control. The issue is "who is going to control your life?"

Being your own person does not have to mean giving up your place in a group. Being your own person means examining and judging something and then deciding what's best for you.

It may be useful to think of the worst case associated with both alternatives. The worst case of saying "no" may be name calling, shaming and ridicule by those applying the pressure, and you feeling left out, not one of the crowd. The worst case of saying "yes," can be addiction, with all its myriad problems, the loss of control of your mind and body, and even death.

When someone tells you "how much fun," or "how great it is to get high," they are telling only a part of the story. If they tell you it's fun and harmless, they are leaving out the part about consequences and lying about harmless. Think about the consequences. They are not fun!

If a friend really cares about you, how you choose to deal with alcohol and other drugs will not affect the friendship. If your abstinence negatively affects the friendship, then the person cares more about you being like them, than about you.

Recognize that those applying pressure are often doing so because of fear or guilt. They may realize that what they are doing is wrong and they may fear that you will reveal to others what they are doing. Or, they may secretly feel guilty and will feel better if you and everyone else is doing what they are doing. Don't let their problems become your problems.

You will inevitably be tempted to go along. There are some fundamental things you can do to maintain control: 1. Prepare, 2. Develop a Support Network, 3. Exercise Your Right to Choose.

Effectively dealing with the pressure takes forethought and planning. Be prepared ahead of time, so you don't do something you will regret. Always consider the consequences. Think it through. Develop a plan for what you will say and do, when being pressured. It is easier to say no if you know <u>why</u> you are saying no.

Two fundamental strategies for dealing with peer pressure involve avoiding it. You do that by: 1. Carefully selecting those with whom you choose to associate. Spend your time only with people you want to be like. 2. Avoiding situations where pressure might be applied. If you know that a planned gathering is likely to involve drugs and alcohol, don't go.

If you find yourself in situations where pressure is being applied, other ways of coping without caving include:

- It is almost always better <u>not</u> to attempt to argue the merits of the action. That can be interpreted as judgmental by the person(s) applying the pressure, those who clearly plan to participate. If you criticize imbibing, they are likely to take it as criticism of them personally. It's better to just say "it's not for me."
- Have a list of excuses prepared. Blame your refusal on parents, coaches, you have to be somewhere, etc.
- Home Drug Test Kits are now readily available. Tell your "friend" that your parents/coach, are doing random drug testing and you will be in big trouble if you are caught. (grounded, loss of privileges, kicked off the team, etc.).
- Not tonight. I'm not feeling well.
- Suggest an alternative activity. If someone wants to drink or do drugs, propose some other idea for spending the time.
- Attempt to diffuse the pressure by asking lots of questions and then saying "I need to think about it."
- Simply leave the scene.
- Stretch the truth: "I'm allergic to alcohol. I took a shot once. It made my skin blotchy and caused me to vomit." "I'm allergic to pot. I smoked a joint once and it made me puke."
- Find a friend who shares your position and back each other up.

- Don't fall for the line that "everybody's doing it." Everybody is not doing it.
- Don't ride with someone who has been drinking alcohol or doing drugs. Find an alternative, even if it's walking. Don't put your life in danger for fear of offending someone.

Develop a code, a signal, with your parents. Agree that if you say a certain word or phrase on the telephone, they will ask your location and come pick you up, with no questions asked. Tell your "friends" that your mom/dad just called and something has come up at home, and they are coming to pick you up.

Test your decisions about yielding to peer pressure against your values and goals. Ask yourself if doing what you are being urged to do conflicts with who you want to be. Remember that your life is more important than what your "friends" think of you. You have lots of things to do.

Identify a network of friends, family and adults you admire and trust to provide support. When faced with a tempting situation, think about what these people would suggest you do. (What would _____ suggest I do in this situation?).

True friends do not pressure friends to do things that are potentially harmful. If your friends do that, find some new friends. Drugs regularly destroy goals and dreams. Don't sacrifice yours for a temporary "rush."

Recognize that peer pressure can be a factor in decisions about subjects other than harmful substances. Some think that shoplifting is a thrill. Some will encourage you to join in taunting and ridiculing someone who is different. While I was preparing this book, an article in our newspaper told the story of a local 14-year-old girl who committed suicide as a result of intense and repeated bullying by her classmates. This is just one example of the sad consequences of unhealthy peer pressure.

It's your life. You have the right to choose. Exercise it. Dealing with peer pressure is a skill. Like any other skill it takes preparation and practice. If an activity is not "right," choose not to participate.

The decision to "do" drugs can have devastating results. The choice is yours. Only you are responsible for you. When making a decision about harmful substances, remember to ask yourself if the choice fits with who you want to be. If you've started, you can stop. Find a counselor to help you stop. If you haven't started, think about the risks. Choose wisely.

The greatest travesty in America today is the lives ruined and/or lost due to drugs, alcohol and nicotine. The temporary "high" or satisfying the craving are not worth the consequences.

Please carefully consider taking the pledge outlined in Appendix I. Note that this is a pledge you make to yourself. No one needs to know which lines you checked or if you signed it. It is your choice. You need not show it to anyone. If you trust someone to keep you accountable, share it with that person.

A fundamental element of character is keeping commitments you make to yourself. This is an important one.

Just say NO!

The substances mentioned in this section can kill you, and/or ruin your life, literally and totally. It's not worth the risk. Choose to exclude them.

If you are already involved, and would like help in dealing with tobacco, drugs, or alcohol, call the Center for Substance Abuse at 1-800-662 4357, or Alateen at 1-888-425-2666.

Please read and reflect on the situation outlined in Case Study 10, "Weed or Ball," at the end of this chapter. Consider what you would do in Brett's situation.

So far we've considered the foundations for living an effective life and examined the impact of a couple of major decision areas. Almost all decisions affect our lives in some way. Next we'll look at how we can improve the decision making process, to achieve better results.

CASE STUDY 9 - IS THE THRILL WORTH THE PRICE?

Eight teenagers were sprawled on the couches in the counseling center. There was no joking or hassling one another. They did not want to be there. Neither did the counselor. He was charged with helping these young people cope with a tragedy. Three of their classmates had died in an auto accident following a beer party intended to celebrate their upcoming graduation. They were drunk.

The youth in the room had been through counseling, sermons, and lectures over the previous four days. They were still dazed. It all seemed so overwhelming. They had listened to multiple testimonies about what great kids the deceased were. They had heard the chief of police relate that one never gets used to, or forgets, the horror on the faces of parents when you break the news to them that their child is gone forever.

The counselor was at a loss as to what to do or say that hadn't already been said. Finally, he related a personal story. He told them that when he was their age he saw in a shop window a motor bike like he had always wanted. It was beautiful, and he had to have it. He was stunned at the price, but didn't let that stop him. He had to have that bike. He stripped his savings, that he had been accumulating for specific purchases, and borrowed some money from his dad.

The students looked at him dumbfounded. What did this story have to do with their grief?

He explained that in subsequent months, after buying the bike, he realized that what he had to give up, including a graduation class ring for himself, and buying a nice birthday present for his girlfriend, made the price for the bike too high. It hadn't been worth it.

He told the young people that he learned from that experience that it is always wise to weigh benefits versus the price in all situations. He said that he subsequently realized that this cost vs benefits principle applied to actions as well as purchases. He gently pointed out that the "cost" of the good times their friends had at the party was just too high.

One boy observed that we often don't know what the price is in advance. Maybe nothing bad will happen, even if we take a risk.

"That is true", replied the counselor, we often don't know the consequences in advance, but we can evaluate the situation, think about what the consequences could be, and what the probabilities are, before we make a choice.

The counselor then asked if they could think of anything good that might come out of the tragedy, or if they should just try to forget it, like it was a sad movie.

One of the girls timidly suggested that they could maybe make a pledge, or something.

Another girl suggested that the pledge might include something like imagining there is a price tag on the things parents think we shouldn't do, so we can decide if we are willing to pay that price if we do it anyway.

"I'll buy that," one of the boys chimed in.

The group started working on the wording of a pledge to which they would be willing to commit.

Does the concept of weighing benefits versus costs make sense to you?

What do you think might be appropriate to include in the pledge the group is preparing?

What other things might the group do to make something good come out of the tragedy?

CASE STUDY 10 - WEED OR BALL

My name is Brett. I grew up with a bunch of friends. We were really close. We did lots of things together. We went to the same school. We'd go to movies, hang at the local sandwich shop and play video games at each other's houses. Our favorite thing was playing basketball at the city park. We had an unofficial team and would occasionally play against a group from another school.

Don was the leader of the group. He had a great sense of humor and he was like the unofficial peacekeeper. Whenever there were differences, he would get them ironed out. We were close friends.

We had great times, until, when we were about 14, one of the guys suggested that we pool our money and buy some weed. I didn't want to have anything to do with weed, because I had read what it could do to you. I told them I didn't have any money, thinking that if I didn't put in money, they wouldn't let me smoke. But they had enough money and said I could smoke anyway.

We were in the park, and one guy lit the joint, took a puff, and passed it around. As it was going around, I tried to figure out what I was going to do. I watched the others. Everyone coughed hard after they took a puff. I was at the end of the line. I said "Chill, I don't want any."

"Take a puff son. It's mad nice."
"If you don't smoke, you're a herb."
"You can't be mamma's boy the rest of your life."

I was tempted, but came to my senses and passed it on.

"You really are a herb."

When they had finished smoking several blunts, they started acting like fools. They were hitting each other and saying stupid things. Seeing the way they acted, made me glad I hadn't smoked.

The next day, they all talked about how lousy they felt. You would think that might make them come to their senses, but they immediately started planning how they could get more.

Over the past year, smoking weed has become a regular thing, and it has changed them. They always look like zombies. Their eyes are red and puffy. They have bad tempers and are always ready to fight. Don has changed the most. He has the baddest temper of them all. Once, when we were playing basketball, I accidentally hit him on the hand. He exploded. "Why the hell are you fouling me?" I said it was an accident. He tried to punch me, but missed.

A week later I called Don's house. His mom said he was at the park. I went to the park and saw all the guys just finishing a game against the kids from another school. When the game was over, I asked Don why he hadn't told me about the game. He said, "Since you think you're too good for us, we didn't think you wanted to be on the team."

I couldn't believe it! I had been kicked off the team, because I refused to smoke weed.

Being rejected by my friends makes me think that, "maybe I should smoke just one time so they will like me, and let me be part of the team." I don't know what to do.

Why are Brett's friends trying to get him to smoke pot?

What is their purpose in calling him names?

Why have they excluded him from the group?

If Brett, as he is thinking, smokes one time to gain acceptance, will that solve his problem?

What should Brett do?

PART III - HOW TO MAKE BETTER DECISIONS

CHAPTER 6 - CHOICES MATTER

Decision-making is the most important thing you do. When considering important choices, ask yourself: "Does this choice reflect <u>who</u> I want to be?" You create yourself through the decisions you make. Every important choice you make is a decision, not only about what to do, but a decision about **Who You Are**.

Be Careful About Assumptions

It was the last day of school before Christmas break and the third-grade class was having a party. The teacher was making a game of trying to guess what was in the gift boxes the students had brought for her.

To the little girl whose parents owned a candy store, she said "is it chocolates?" The girl responded "yes."

To the boy whose parents owned a flower shop, she asked "is it roses?" The boy indicated that it was.

(continued below)

Decisions drive everything. Decisions determine whether our nation goes to war and sends our young people off to fight and die. Decisions determine whether our economy grows or stagnates. Decisions determine whether our planet can continue to support life as we know it. Our fate is determined by our personal decisions, by the decisions of elected officials, bureaucrats, corporate executives and others in positions of influence. The choices we make when we vote at the ballot box, and when we express our opinions; with our voices, with our feet and with our spending money, all matter. The future of our economy, our country, and our planet will be determined by the quality of individual and collective human decisions.

> When the boy whose father operated a beer/wine carry-out presented his box, she noticed that there was liquid leaking from the package. She dabbed her finger in the moisture and tasted it. Not recognizing the taste, she asked if it was champagne. The boy said no. She tasted the liquid again and asked if it was some other kind of wine. No exclaimed the excited boy. "It's a puppy!"

We make hundreds of decisions every day. Many are not earth shaking – What should I wear today? Which cereal should I have for breakfast? Some, however, are life-changing - What career should I pursue? Should I go into debt to attend college? Is that person the right spouse for me? Should I "try" addictive substances? Unfortunately, other than perhaps "fretting" a little more, we often approach important decisions much like we do minor decisions.

Decisions made today may impact your life for years down the road. Choosing the wrong <u>vacation</u> will likely have minimal impact in the long run. Choosing the wrong <u>vocation</u> can make your life miserable. Evaluating the importance of decisions is critical.

Although decision - making is among the most frequent things we do, and certainly among the **most important things we do**, we are not typically taught how to do it, nor do most of us consciously make an effort to learn how to do it. We are presumably supposed to learn decision-making by observation or through experience. Observing the results of other people's decisions can be helpful, but observation, by itself, does not work well for learning how to make decisions. And while experience, "the school of hard knocks," can provide useful lessons, it is very inefficient and often painful when it is the only method of learning.

Important decisions, those that have significant ramifications for you and for others, warrant focused time and effort. Decision-making is a <u>critical life skill</u>. Fortunately, it's a skill that can be learned and improved. You can learn to be a better decision-maker. Like learning to drive a car, it can be awkward at first, but you get more proficient with practice. To make better decisions, you have to **want** to learn, and to grow in proficiency.

Not all decisions are of a "yes or no", "black or white" type. Most important decisions involve shades of gray. Most must be made with less than all the information that may be relevant. Many must be made under time and/or other pressures. Some involve trade-offs between conflicting objectives or rules. In spite of all these obstacles, learning to make effective choices, with the information and time available, is possible, and can be very rewarding.

While the purpose of decision-making is usually to produce positive results, outcomes are often uncertain. Even with the careful application of the best process, there is no guarantee that the results of a given decision will be positive. Good decisions can have negative consequences and poor decisions, by chance or luck, can be followed by great results. Following an effective process will, in the long run, produce better results than knee jerk reactions and hap-hazard approaches.

Always take responsibility for the decisions you make, and don't abdicate decisions that should be yours. It's your life. You are the one who should, whenever possible, make the decisions that affect it. Be sensitive to the significance of your decisions and develop the self-discipline to invest in each decision the effort it warrants. You take constructive ownership of your life through the choices you make.

You can learn to make better decisions by: becoming more aware of their impact on your life, taking responsibility for your decisions, consciously committing to improving them, developing a truthful and realistic understanding of the world within which you make decisions, and employing an effective decision-making process. We will take a look at process next.

CHAPTER 7 - DEVELOP AN EFFECTIVE DECISION-MAKING PROCESS

Making better decisions requires both intention and attention. Effective decision making starts with awareness. Be aware that a decision is required and give the decision the attention it deserves. Decision making is a critical life skill, a skill that can never be perfected, but can be developed and significantly enhanced. You can make better decisions, if you want to do so enough to work at it. The meaning of your life, your achievements, your happiness and your self-satisfaction all depend largely upon the choices you make. Recognize that this is so, and treat decision making accordingly.

Understand that no one makes <u>only</u> good decisions. Your objective should be, not to make "perfect" decisions every time, but to <u>make "better" decisions more often</u>. Following a systematic, logical process and consciously attempting to think rationally can help significantly.

An effective process + wisdom = better decisions. Better decisions = a better quality of life.

Effectively making important decisions can be tough and the consequences serious. Most of our more serious life problems are the result of poor decisions. Our prisons are full of people who made poor choices.

Many of our poor decisions are the result of not understanding **how** to make effective decisions. The quality of our decisions is determined by **what** we decide. What we decide is determined, in part, by **how** we decide. The process is important. Using an effective process will not make tough decisions easy, but it will provide the assurance that you have given the issue your best effort and will increase the probability of a successful outcome.

Identify the key elements of the issue, gather relevant information, apply rigorous analysis and make the decision. The following is an outline of a systematic approach to improving decision-making. Each step is explained below.

A PROCESS FOR MAKING EFFECTIVE DECISIONS

1. FRAME (DEFINE) THE ISSUE
2. IDENTIFY AND GATHER THE INFORMATION NEEDED TO MAKE A GOOD DECISION
3. IDENTIFY VIABLE OPTIONS/ALTERNATIVES
4. CONSIDER THE LIKELY CONSEQUENCES/RESULTS
5. CONSIDER THE IMPACT ON OTHERS
6. TEST THE ALTERNATIVES AGAINST YOUR VALUES
7. TEST THE ALTERNATIVES AGAINST YOUR GOALS AND OBJECTIVES
8. TUNE IN TO YOUR INTUITION
9. THINK IT THROUGH
10. MAKE A DECISION
11. IMPLEMENT IT
12. EVALUATE PAST DECISIONS

Should you consciously apply each of these steps to every decision you make? Of course not, life is too short. They are intended for major decisions, and as aids, not rigid requirements.

The focus of this section is on improving the quality of critical, significant, and important decisions. Through employing this process for those, you will come to naturally apply the principles and the mental discipline to your mundane, routine decisions, and inevitably improve the quality of those as well.

The dominant excuse for not employing an effective process in decision-making is the **"I don't have time"** rationalization. There is a lot of truth to the old adage that "if you don't take time to do it right the first time, you will have to take time to do it over again." The key is to match the time and effort you invest in the decision to the importance of the issue and the potential impact of the consequences. Make the time to give important decisions the attention and effort they warrant.

Time can have a major impact on the quality of decisions. We rarely have all the time we would like for considering important decisions. Procrastination almost always has negative consequences. Putting off decisions, until there is little time for analysis and thinking, often leads to poor choices and may mean that the best alternatives are no longer available.

While employing an effective process is very important, it is not the only determinant of the quality of decisions. **The wisdom you bring to the process, your attitude, knowledge, experience, and mindset have a significant impact on the effectiveness of your decisions.** We will examine these factors in Parts IV and V.

GUIDELINES for IMPLEMENTING THE TWELVE STEPS

1. Frame the Issue

    What's it all about? The first step in the decision-making process is to define or "frame" the issue. I use the word "issue" instead of "problem" on purpose. Much of what is written about decision-making stresses "problem-solving", and often equates decision making with problem-solving. While problem-solving requires effective decision-making skills, not all decisions involve problems. The word "problem" has a negative connotation not always useful to the process. Choosing between alternative job offers, both significantly better than your current job, is not a "problem". Choosing which of two good used cars to buy, is not a problem. We should view decisions, not as problems, but as <u>opportunities</u> of two kinds: the opportunity to make the best of the issue at hand, and the opportunity to practice, (and thus improve), our decision-making skills. Defining the essence and scope of the issue is the foundation of a useful process.

Defining the issue involves answering some basic questions:

　　a.　Why is a decision required?
　　b.　What is the real issue?
　　c.　What are the root causes of the issue/problem?
　　d.　How important is the decision?
　　e.　What are the real needs associated with the decision?
　　f.　What is your primary objective? What are your secondary objectives?
　　g.　What are the primary, real constraints?
　　h.　What are your wants/preferences associated with the decision
　　i.　By when should the decision be made?

Why Is a Decision Required? Identifying why a decision is required helps define the issue and assists with answering other framing questions. "My teacher told me that he wants my project turned in by Monday, or I will get zero credit," is a legitimate consideration when deciding how you are going to spend your weekend. It also establishes a deadline. Understanding why you are making the decision will help you make better decisions.

What Is the Real Issue? Issues sometimes wear disguises. Developing the perfect solution to the wrong issue is not useful. Definition is critical. The way you define an issue can significantly influence your choices. A question of "Should I buy the Sony or Samsung big screen TV?," might more legitimately be defined as "Should I make such a purchase at all?"

Writing down your issue definition is critical. It forces you to think it through. An "Issue Definition Worksheet" to help with defining the scope of the decision issue is provided in Appendix J.

> *The formulation of a problem is often more essential than its solution.*   - Albert Einstein

What Is the Root Cause? If the issue is not a problem, why did the issue come up? If it is a problem, what is the root cause (or causes)? It is often useful to utilize the elementary technique of asking: "Why, Who, What, Where, When, and How."

How Important Is the Decision? A fundamental issue is deciding how much time and effort to invest in a decision, and how rigorously to apply the chosen process. The more critical the consequences, the more you should invest in the effort. To facilitate the process, a system for assigning rankings can be useful:

  a. Critical - These are the life-altering decisions that deserve your best efforts. (post high school education choices, career choices, spouse choices, choices about addictive substances, etc.).
  b. Significant - These are the choices that have a major impact on the quality of your life, but are not likely to completely change it. (Buying a home in the suburbs or renting an apartment in the city, etc.).
  c. Material – These make a difference, but don't have a major impact. (Choosing a dude ranch or a beach resort for the next family vacation, etc.).

    d. Mundane – These are the trivial choices we make every day. (What to have for lunch, which shoes to put on, etc.). They do not deserve a rigorous application of the process because the consequences don't matter much.

What Are the Real Needs? Distinguish between wants and needs. What results are really necessary to solve the problem or resolve the issue? Needs are basic. They represent what is required. The key is focus. For the best results, focus on the real needs. The more clearly you see the <u>results</u> you <u>need</u>, the easier it will be to identify and evaluate choices, and thus make an effective decision.

What Are Your Objectives? Objectives should address the real needs. Objectives define <u>results</u> to be accomplished in specific, measurable terms, with specified due dates clearly stated. Objectives help us identify what information we need, channel the development of alternatives and provide standards against which to test potential choices. It is not unusual to identify multiple objectives for major decisions. Prioritize objectives in terms of importance. Identify all your objectives, even those that conflict. You will need to address any conflicts in the analysis phase. Write down all that you hope to accomplish by making this decision.

What Are the Real Constraints? There are typically factors that limit the range of feasible choices. Money is a common constraint. A cap on the dollars available can limit the options. Time and geography can narrow the list of practical alternatives. Determine which constraints are "real". Question every identified constraint to determine if it is in fact restrictive or merely a "mental" barrier, a result of having limited vision. Brainstorm how constraints might be removed, or rendered inconsequential.

What Are Your Wants/Preferences? As humans, our emotions are real and relevant. That's ok. Making good decisions sometimes means resolving conflicts between wants and needs and thus requires tough choices. We should distinguish needs from wants, but it is unwise to treat decision-making so mechanically that you ignore your emotions or the emotions of those affected by the decision. It is better to consciously acknowledge and consider your personal feelings and their impact on your choices, than to have them unconsciously bias your thinking.

When? By when must the decision be made? Time is often a critical factor, sometimes imposed by others or by circumstances. Identify precisely when a decision must be made, and schedule backward from there. Hard decisions deserve ample time for analysis. When dealing with important decisions, allow sufficient time to utilize the process. When circumstances permit, take control of the schedule and allow enough time to prepare for making the choice. Don't procrastinate until time pressures force you into making a poor or less than optimal choice. Putting off the analysis and the decision can mean that some attractive alternatives are no longer available, or that someone else makes the decision for you. Give yourself a deadline.

Time and effort spent accurately defining/framing the decision issue will save time in the long run and provide a firm foundation for improving the quality of your decisions. Be thorough in defining the issue. Restate it in a number of different ways, until you are confident that you have it right. The best resolution to the wrong issue is not very helpful.

2. Identify and Gather Relevant Information

   Once you have the issue clearly defined, ask yourself: "What information would be useful for making this decision?" Make a list of what you really need. For important decisions, it would be unusual for you to have in your memory bank everything necessary for making an effective decision. Additional information is usually required. Information is of three kinds:

   - Critical – Information without which the decision should not be made (if at all possible).
   - Useful – Information it would be beneficial to have, if time permits.
   - Irrelevant – any and all information that has no impact on the decision.

   It is important to distinguish among the three types, to give priority to the critical and to refuse to spend time chasing the irrelevant.

   Relevant information can be "hard," i.e. facts and figures, and "emotional" – how you feel about the issue and why you feel that way are valid considerations. Both hard and emotional issues are important. Don't ignore either. It is especially useful to ask yourself why you feel the way you do about a subject. What is the source of your feelings? Consider how those affected by the decision are likely to feel about the issue. That nagging feeling may be your conscience telling you "something is not right here."

   There are myriad sources of information: books, articles, the internet, experts (authorities respected in their fields) and personal observations/experience. Use them. Whenever possible and practical, verify what you read or hear before giving it credibility.

Be selective. Do not accumulate data for the sake of data or to put off having to make the decision. Develop, refine and use your list of what you really need.

> *It is of the highest importance in the art of detection to be able to recognize, out of a number of facts, which are incidental and which vital.*
>
> — Sherlock Holmes (Arthur Conan Doyle)

Know When to Quit! Deadlines may dictate, but so should judgment. The time spent gathering information should be related to the importance of the decision, and consideration of the "utility" of gathering additional information, i. e. at what point is the value of additional information insufficient to justify the effort to obtain more information? Keep asking yourself if more information will really enable you to make a more effective decision.

3. Identify and Clearly Define Alternatives

After gathering relevant information, it's time to consider potential alternatives. The decision you make can be no better than the best alternative you conjure up, so time spent identifying options is usually well spent. This is an important step. Far too many decisions are unsatisfactory because the decision maker failed to consider enough options. Ask yourself "What are the alternative ways that I might meet my objectives?"

   a. Brainstorm. Be creative. There are almost always more options than those that initially come to mind. Think outside the proverbial "box."
   b. Don't evaluate options while creating. The key to brainstorming effectiveness is to avoid making

judgments when <u>developing</u> alternatives. Get as many options on the table as possible. Postpone critiquing, to prevent stifling creativity.

c. Examine your assumptions about limitations. Some constraints are real, but some are only mental. Imagine that the apparent limitation did not exist. What could you do in that case?

d. Begin early and plan time for breaks in the process. Your subconscious will keep wrestling with the issue and may well come up with a fresh concept.

e. Review your experience. What worked (or didn't work) for you in similar situations? You should learn from all experiences, but don't slip into the rut of considering just the same old alternatives.

f. Aim high. Don't just settle for incremental improvements. Set lofty targets.

g. Imagine what a person you admire and respect would do in your situation.

h. Think for yourself first, and then seek suggestions from one or more persons you admire and respect. Sometimes the process of explaining the issue you are facing to someone else will stimulate you to come up with a new possibility. A different perspective can be helpful, but never abdicate the development of your alternatives list.

i. Keep reviewing your list. Any one idea may spark a thought about a related possibility.

j. Consider combining alternatives to develop an even better one.

Whatever the process you use for generating alternatives, list several options that have a reasonable chance of working. Thinking through a comprehensive list helps you avoid impulsively pursuing the first idea that sounds good, but may not be the <u>best</u> choice. Recognize that you cannot choose an alternative that you have not included in the analysis, and your choice can be no better than the best of those on your list. Identify as many reasonable options as possible.

Think beyond the obvious parameters. Your alternatives should be driven by your objectives, but be sure your framing of the issue is appropriate. You may do a fantastic job of establishing and evaluating just the right alternatives for purchasing a new home in the ideal neighborhood, but if there is a reasonable probability that you will be transferred to another town in the next two years, renting should be included in your list of housing options.

Be very specific about the definition of the alternatives. Think them through and write them down.

4. Consider the Likely Consequences

No one has perfect foresight. It is difficult to predict the outcomes of possible choices. However, to make better decisions, you must make a conscious effort to predict the consequences of your choices. Carefully estimating the probable results of each of your options will help you select the one that best meets your objectives.

The more clearly you understand the issue, your objectives and the consequences of your options, the higher the probability that your choice will be a good one. If you have accurately defined the consequences of your options, your decision will sometimes become obvious, without further analysis.

While reflecting upon your careful definition of the issue and your specifically stated objectives:

a. Reject any that are clearly inferior. Refine your list of options to a manageable number, perhaps three to five. Winnowing out those inconsistent with real constraints can help narrow the list. Ranking and prioritizing can help as well.
b. Attempt to imagine the most likely implications of choosing each of these short list alternatives. Write them down. Be very realistic, specific, and accurate. Don't kid yourself.
c. Consider the long term-impact of each of the options. Imagine how you would feel about the choice in a year, three years, ten years.
d. Use the hard data developed in your information search, but reflect on it with logic and judgment.
e. Identify and acknowledge uncertainties. You won't know the consequences for sure until after the decision.
f. Ask yourself: What has to happen or not happen for this situation to turn out well? What are the consequences of being wrong?
g. Ask yourself if you can live with what might realistically be a worst-case scenario.
h. Consult with authorities you respect. A professional in the field (law, finance, medicine) may have a better grasp of the consequences of certain types of decisions than you. For less technical issues, a trusted friend might serve as a useful sounding board.
i. Whenever possible, use measurements that are objective, and meaningful and that reflect a reasonable level of precision for the subject being evaluated.
j. Narrow the list of options to those that come closest to meeting your objectives.

Keeping variables organized mentally is a challenge. It is almost always more effective to write things down. This is especially true when attempting comparisons. A worksheet like the one in Appendix K can be very helpful for visualizing and organizing information about possible consequences.

5. Consider the Impact On Others

People Matter! When considering the consequences of alternative decisions, pay particular attention to the consequences for others. Our decisions rarely affect only us. Think through who will be influenced by your decision and how they will be affected. Your choices can change lives, and not just your own. To help you understand the implications for others, write down the names of those likely to be impacted by your important decisions and the likely positive and negative effects on their lives.

Some decisions involve sacrifices. You may be perfectly willing to make personal sacrifices to take on and complete some task, because you value what you perceive to be the end result. Think carefully about the sacrifices others will have to make if you decide to pursue a particular course of action. Others who will be affected may not see the long-term benefits that you see, or care as much about the outcome as you do. They may not be willing to make the sacrifices your decision will require of them.

Put yourself in the shoes of those who will be impacted by your choice. Treat them the way you would like to be treated.

When major decisions will impact others, get them involved in the process. Let them know what you are thinking. Share relevant information. Ask for, and listen to, input. Demonstrate a willingness to consider ideas and alternatives suggested by others. This does not mean that such decisions should always be made by consensus or majority vote. You should not abdicate decisions. Even if you have to make an unpopular decision, you will receive less resistance and more cooperation and commitment if those affected are informed and involved.

Using a worksheet like that in Appendix L can be helpful for considering the impact on others.

6. Test Possible Choices Against Your Values

   Several years ago, Tony Campolo, a noted author who was the key speaker at a leadership conference I attended, related some research in which a group of mothers of Japanese children were asked: "if you could be granted one wish for your child, for what would you wish?" The overwhelming response from that group was that they would wish for their children to be "successful." When a group of American mothers was asked the same question, the overwhelming response was that they would wish for their children to be "happy." The question posed was a question about VALUES. Tony contended that both answers were inappropriate. What we should wish for our children is that they will be "GOOD." Being good means owning and practicing the right values. The virtue of being good applies to all ages.

   In Part I, we talked about how to define develop and clarify personal values. Testing possible choices against your values should be viewed as a critical step in the decision-making process.

7. Test Possible Choices Against Your Personal Goals and Objectives

   Not all your decisions will impact your personal goals and objectives. When one does, it is important to determine the likely implications each choice would have for their attainment. Of course, to test for implications, you must have defined your goals and objectives. If you haven't developed goals and objectives, DO IT NOW, before you have to make the next significant decision in your life. ("How to" guidelines are provided in Part VI).

No matter how attractive a choice may appear in the short run, if it is inconsistent with where you want to go and what you want to be in the long run, it is not likely to be a wise choice.

When evaluating possible decision alternatives, ask yourself what impact that choice is likely to have on the attainment of your personal goals and objectives. Consciously test alternatives against them. This practice becomes an effective means for weeding out unacceptable options and will help keep your life on track.

8. Tune In to Your Intuition

Intuition sometime gets a bad rap because it is 'unscientific." It smacks of "having a hunch about which horse to bet on in the fifth race." It is very important not to confuse hunches with hopes. Do not let what you would <u>like</u> to happen determine what you think <u>will</u> happen.

In fact, intuition accurately defined and applied, can be a great asset for effective decision-making. If intuition is understood as drawing on a synthesis of one's <u>experience</u>, <u>knowledge</u> and <u>values</u> when making decisions, it can be a very useful resource. Intuition can be viewed as using what you know. We sometimes do not realize what all we know. Noted psychologists Carl Jung and Rollo May both wrote of intuition as the unconscious mind delivering data and experiences to the conscious mind. Think of your unconscious mind combing through every relevant experience you have ever had, every relevant fact you have ever learned and every personal value you have established, and sending a summary by email to your conscious mind. Jung described intuition as "an unconscious ability to perceive possibilities, to see the global picture while addressing the local situation." So, intuition can also include concepts of creativity and perspective.

If intuition is to be useful, you must be careful about the facts, experiences, and values stored in your unconscious. Intuition will only be as good as the data that feeds it. The reliability of intuition can be enhanced through research, reading, reflection and meditation.

Give your subconscious/intuition time to work. Start early and schedule intervals in your conscious effort.

Ask yourself: "What is my 'gut' telling me about this choice?"

9. Think It Through

Checking your intuition does not mean that analysis should be ignored. Gathering and analyzing relevant information is crucial. The best approach is to utilize both reasoning and intuition.

Sound reasoning is the <u>non-contradictory integration</u> of evidence, experience, values, knowledge and objectives.

Accurately assessing a situation involves <u>being fully aware</u> of circumstances and alternatives, <u>identifying</u> your choices, <u>applying</u> <u>knowledge, understanding, and educated instincts</u> to your analysis, <u>weighing</u> the implications for others and carefully <u>evaluating</u> the possible consequences. Think it through.

"I think, therefore I am."   - Rene Descartes

This is the point in the process to analyze and evaluate alternatives. Start by reviewing all the previous steps and asking yourself fundamental questions. Appendix M provides a checklist for analyzing/reviewing major decisions to assure that all relevant information has been considered.

Rigorously challenge each of the constraints. Are there ways to mitigate any of them? Reassess the alternatives. Has your work thus far stimulated the possibility of others? Would combining two or more result in a better alternative?

Be particularly sensitive to evidence that indicates an error in your thinking, and be willing to correct such errors. Thinking can change thinking. That is one of the attributes that makes it so powerful.

Make any refinements indicated by this review.

Apply the criteria by which you will evaluate the alternatives. This is an important step, because it forces you to think about what is really important to you and what is really relevant to the decision at hand. Make sure that the criteria accurately reflect your values, goals and concerns for the impact on others

Next, apply sound reasoning to evaluate the alternatives and the anticipated consequences.

Whether or not you use one or more "techniques" described, all steps in the process require judgment. Good judgment comes from values, principles, experience, education, logic and reason. Don't ignore judgment in favor of some formula. Apply good judgment to the process.

10. Make the Decision

The time and effort you spend on various decisions will, and should, vary significantly. Two factors affect the appropriate time and effort involved; the expected consequences of the decision and the amount of time circumstances and pressures permit. Consciously match process time and effort to the impact the decision is likely to have. As soon as you have completed the analysis that the importance of the decision justifies, make the decision. Knowing <u>when</u> to make the decision is a critical element in making better decisions. You will almost never have all the information and time you would like. Reflect carefully on what you have and "pull the trigger."

11. Implement

    Once you have made the decision, develop a plan and implement it. Don't procrastinate. <u>The best decision you can ever conceive is meaningless unless implemented.</u> Identifying the best way to implement it, will likely involve another set of decisions, decisions such as when and how. Apply what you have learned about decision making to the decisions about how to implement.

    Develop an action plan. Write it down.

    The value of a plan comes from engaging in the planning <u>process</u>. It forces you to think. It is unlikely that things will go exactly as planned, but with a plan, you are much better prepared to respond and adapt to the unexpected. The purpose of a plan is not to lock you into a rigid set of steps, but to prepare you to adapt to developments and effectively achieve your objectives. It also establishes a standard, a measuring stick, against which to measure progress and determine completion.

    Ask yourself these questions:

    a. What has to be done to make this decision effective?
    b. Who has to be informed, and of what?
    c. Who has to do what?
    d. From whom do I need assistance?

e. What are the important interim and final completion dates?
  f. What resources/tools are required?
  g. How will I track progress?
  h. How will I measure results?
  i. What are my contingency plans?

For some decisions, implementation is a simple one-step process. You decide and you do it. Others are more complex, involve multiple steps and require the involvement of others. To assist with those, an Implementation Planning Worksheet is provided in Appendix N. Be sure that the action plan includes: periodic checks to see if things are on track, follow up steps that are required, coordination with outside persons or organizations, and a final review to see that all bases have been covered.

Things do not always go as planned. It is useful to think about what you will do if problems arise or things turn out differently than anticipated. Thinking through and developing plans for contingencies can help you adapt if the need arises.

> *I have been impressed with the urgency of doing. Knowing is not enough; we must apply. Being willing is not enough; we must do.* - Leonardo da Vinci

<u>Demonstrate a bias for action. Don't just sit there. Do something.</u>

> *Perhaps the most valuable result of all education is the ability to make yourself do the thing you have to do when it ought to be done, whether you like it or not. It is the first lesson that ought to be learned and, however early a person's training begins, it is probably the last lesson a person learns thoroughly.* - Thomas Henry Huxley

12. Evaluate Past Decisions

Don't succumb to the tendency to ignore or "forget" poor decisions and savor just the good ones. You learn to make decisions by making decisions. You will learn more about making decisions if you keep notes during the process and subsequently analyze both decisions that produced good results and those that did not turn out well. Ask yourself:

a. What was the real reason I chose as I did?
b. What are the real reasons this decision turned out well or poorly?
c. Did I define the issue accurately?
d. Did I consider all the realistic alternatives?
e. What information should I have sought that I didn't?
f. Was the information I used really relevant?
g. Was there a way that I could have more realistically anticipated the consequences?
h. What clues did I miss?
i. What did I learn?
j. Regardless of the results, what should I have done differently in the process?

Keep in mind that you must not judge choices solely by results. The quality of the process counts. "Good" decisions can have poor consequences because of factors beyond your control, and "poor" decisions may turn out well. The objective of the evaluation process is to learn things that will help you make better decisions in the future.

> *Some of the best lessons we ever learn are learned from past mistakes. The error of the past is the wisdom and enabler of the future.* - Dale Turner

Acknowledge your effective decisions. Reflecting on the positives helps build confidence and self-esteem, which leads to better decision-making. Ask: "What did I learn that I can apply in the future?" Analyze, don't rationalize, the dysfunctional ones. Ask: "What did I learn that I can apply in the future?"

Don't use the evaluation to beat yourself up for mistakes, but to improve your skills for making future decisions. You will never bat 100%, but, over time, making good choices will lead to better consequences and good decisions will lead to more good decisions.

Also bear in mind that it is not at all practical to review every decision. This analysis should be reserved for important decisions, those that have significant consequences.

> *A man who has committed a mistake and doesn't correct it, is making another mistake.*   - Confucius

Using the Decision Log provided in Appendix O is a useful way to evaluate past decisions. Consider developing an 8 ½" X 11" template, making multiple copies, and keeping them in a loose-leaf notebook to help you review and learn from your experience with major decisions.

Deal with Procrastination

Procrastination is the single greatest obstacle to effective decision-making. Sometimes just getting started is the biggest hurtle. Start when you have enough time to complete the process. Allow time during the process to reflect, and to allow your sub-conscious to work. Avoid *analysis paralysis*. Don't get so bogged down in gathering and evaluating information that time and effort is wasted, and/or time sensitive, viable, and attractive alternatives are no longer available. Know when to start and when to quit.

Understand that not choosing is a choice. The opportunity may be missed or someone else may make the choice for you. Not deciding frequently leads to unsatisfactory outcomes. Take control. Make your own decisions.

A major reason for procrastination is FEAR.

- *Fear of Failure* – Some people have difficulties making decisions because they fear making the wrong decision. If you have followed an effective process and thought it through carefully, you have done the best you can do. Some of your decisions will fail. That is inevitable because you are human, but a majority of your choices will be good ones. Don't let fear of making the wrong choice keep you from making a choice. When you make a mistake, learn from it and move on.

- *Fear of the Unknown* – Some have difficulties dealing with uncertainty. The future is uncertain. Focus on what you do know, gather information and rely on experts to fill the gaps. Keep moving toward your goals.

- *Fear of Change* - Some people are uncomfortable with change. They fear that change may mean they lose control.

- *Fear of Rejection* – We hate to hear the word "no." We tend to take a "no" response to an idea, suggestion or choice very personally, interpreting it as a rejection of ourselves, as well as the idea. Some go to great lengths to avoid hearing a "no," avoiding making decisions that might elicit a negative response. Listen carefully to a "no" response. Ask why. There may be valid reasons that you hadn't considered, and should take into account. Modifications may lead to a "yes." Don't let the possibility of a negative response deter you from making a decision.

Focus On What Is Important. There are typically only a few really important elements to a decision. Concentrate on the core issues. Ask yourself: What are the make-or-break elements of this decision? When having difficulty making a decision, ask yourself: "What's bothering me?" "What is it about this situation that is keeping me from promptly making the decision?" The answers will likely indicate where you should focus your attention.

It's important to understand the interconnectivity of decisions. Decisions affect other decisions. The fundamental decisions you make about the really important elements of life - values, principles, morals, goals and objectives, relationships, your worldviews, priorities and attitudes, - all profoundly affect the other choices you make. Making effective decisions about these elements, leads to better choices in all aspects of your life.

CASE STUDY 11 – COMMITMENT TO CONVICTIONS

"I'm sorry Dad, I know I should have told you, ... but... but,"

"But you were scared to tell me, right?"

I hadn't thought about it that way, but I had to admit he was right.

He kept his eyes on the road. "My son, not afraid of the police, their billy-clubs, dogs, and fire hoses, but afraid of his own father. That doesn't seem right." He sighed and looked up the road.

"This marching thing, is like a red flag to a bull. It's asking for trouble, and you right in the middle of it. That's not my way. It's mighty hard for me to swallow. If I had known, I would have told you, no. You and me, we've got to settle this non-violence thing, once and for all."

What did he mean? I had taken a vow to protest injustice, using non-violent methods, just like Martin Luther King Jr. asked us to do. What would I do if my dad ordered me not to get involved?

"You're only fifteen. You're old enough to learn your own way of doing things, but it certainly isn't my way. I think it's wrong. It has already gotten young people killed."

"If I said to you, I admire what you are trying to do, but I don't want you mixed up in it, what would you do?"

"Dad, I wouldn't want to disobey you."

"Dammit, don't be wishy-washy. I asked you, man to man, if I told you not to get involved in this protesting thing, what would you do?"

"I'd tell you I was sorry to disobey… and then I think I'd go ahead…. I feel like I just have to."

"Even though it might get you hurt or killed, you'd still do it?"

"Yes sir."

"Well a man has to do what he has to do."

My dad was calling me a man. Wow!

"You have your ways and I have mine. But if you are determined to put yourself in harm's way, and I can't stop you, I'll have to go with you."

"Sir?"

"I said, I'll have to go with you."

What values, principles and character traits are demonstrated by the son?

What values, principles and character traits are demonstrated by the father?

If you were the son, what would you do?

What effect do you think that this exchange will have on the future relationship of father and son?

Both made important decisions. What influenced the decisions of each?

PART IV – CONSIDER YOUR PERSPECTIVES

Our perceptions of how the world functions and what is important, particularly our perceptions about people, affect the decisions we make and our satisfaction with life.

One of the requirements of living fully is seeking to understand the reasons for our beliefs. Our actions are driven by our perceptions, of which we may or may not be aware. We need to consciously determine our ideas about: what is really important in life, how people should relate to one another, what is right and what is wrong, what is good and what is evil, what constitutes justice and what gives meaning to life. You need to critically examine your perceptions and ensure that they are really yours, not borrowed unconsciously from others.

CHAPTER 8 – EXAMINE YOUR WORLDVIEW

The more accurate your worldview, the closer it aligns with reality, the better your decisions will be, and the more stable your life will be. There are many facets to a personal worldview. The concept includes one's knowledge, philosophy, attitudes, principles, values, emotions, morality, ethics, biases, and more.

The following are observations about some of the more important elements of a worldview, elements that should be given serious thought, because they can have a huge impact on choices, life outcomes, and your satisfaction with life.

A. Human Nature and Human Rights

Philosophers have debated for centuries, (with no consensus), the issue of whether humankind is basically good and altruistic or basically selfish and evil. We will not attempt to resolve that debate, but will instead focus on what assumptions lead to the most effective decisions. Someone who views people as basically "good", and of inherent worth, will make different decisions than one who views people as inherently "evil" and "out to take advantage of me." I personally prefer the conclusions of Mencius, a Chinese philosopher of the Confucian school, who contended that humans have four basic tendencies:

1. A sense of compassion that develops into benevolence.
2. A sense of shame and distain that develops into righteousness.
3. A sense of respect and courtesy that develops into propriety.
4. A sense of right and wrong that develops into wisdom.

He concludes that, humans have the capacity to be good, even though they are not always good.

I like the idea that we have the capacity to be good, but have to choose to exercise that capacity. For decision-making, I suggest that it is appropriate to recognize that all others have that capacity, and until experience indicates otherwise, assume that they have chosen to exercise it.

We should also recognize that all humans have the right to "life, liberty and the pursuit of happiness," and the right to be treated with dignity and respect.

B. Develop a Positive Worldview

"Positive thinking" has gotten a lot of ink since Norman Vincent Peale published his book, *The Power of Positive Thinking,* in 1952. The concept is dismissed by some as unrealistically "looking at the world through rose colored glasses," and ignoring the negative aspects of life. That is unfortunate because it really means approaching life's challenges with a positive attitude. It means trying to see the good in other people, considering yourself and your capabilities as worthy, and attempting to make the best of bad situations.

Studies have shown that those with positive attitudes toward life are typically healthier and happier than those with negative attitudes. These are real benefits, and recent research indicates that there are also positive implications for decision-making.

> **Think Positively**
>
> Define an optimist –
>
> A student who looks in his wallet expecting to find money.

Psychological research at the University of North Carolina demonstrated that experiencing positive thoughts and emotions enabled participants to visualize and articulate more possibilities and alternatives than those with negative thoughts and emotions. This has implications for the process of searching for alternatives and options when making decisions. The same research also indicates that a positive attitude helps one build skill sets (like decision-making and problem-solving skills), that have long range benefits.

A Point to Ponder: Have you ever witnessed someone experiencing negative consequences because of a negative attitude?

A positive mindset makes you feel better and helps you make better choices. Think Positively!

C. Scarcity or Abundance

The concepts of Scarcity and Abundance Mindsets were, if not coined, at least widely publicized by Stephen Covey in his best-selling book: *THE 7 HABITS of HIGHLY EFFECTIVE PEOPLE*. In that book, Covey wrote:

Most people are deeply scripted in what I call the Scarcity Mentality. They see life as having only so much, as though there was only one pie out there, and if someone else were to get a big piece of the pie, it would mean less for everybody else. The Scarcity Mentality is a zero-sum paradigm of life.

Those with a scarcity mindset are convinced that there is simply not enough to go around. Their perception is that if they are to get "more", they have to take it away from someone else. If someone else gets "more", that means there is "less" for them. The scarcity mindset focuses on the short term and ignores the long term. It fosters selfishness and competitiveness rather than collaboration. It creates feelings of jealousy and sadness at another's success or gain.

About the Abundance Mindset, Covey wrote:

The Abundance Mindset, on the other hand, flows from a deep inner sense of personal worth and security. It is the paradigm that there is plenty out there and enough to spare for everybody. It results in the sharing of prestige, of recognition, of profits, of decision-making. It opens possibilities, options, alternatives and creativity.

Peter Diamandis and Steven Kotler in their book, appropriately titled *ABUNDANCE*, convincingly contend that the Scarcity Mentality is not only fallacious, but effectively stifles creativity, as well as solutions to significant world problems. It is a self-fulfilling mindset. The beliefs that: the hole is too deep to climb out of, the problems are too big to solve, the trends are worsening instead of improving, etc., cause many to give up hope, and thus these beliefs get in the way of finding effective solutions. They foster an attitude of "Why should I care?, the world is going to hell anyway."

The authors point out that because we are hard wired to be alert to, and respond instinctively to, threats (a condition necessary for the survival of our ancestors), and because we are constantly bombarded with "bad news," (bad news sells newspapers and air time), we have a negative cognitive bias – the tendency to give more weight to negative information and experiences than positive ones.

> *The inability of people to see the positive trends through the sea of bad news – may be the biggest stumbling block on the road toward abundance.*

Diamandis and Kotler argue that the world's major problems are solvable. What it takes is a different way of framing the issues and visualizing solutions.

There is plenty of "good" for everyone. Resolve to be a part of the solution, not a part of the problem. Think WIN/WIN! Think ABUNDANCE!

D. Who Is In Control?

Clinical psychologist Julian Rotter found that those who understood that they had internal control over their lives, versus a belief that external forces controlled their lives, had significantly higher levels of personal achievement, success, and happiness. Those operating on the internal control end of the spectrum experience the most positive results.

Rotter found that people with a more internal sense of control:

1. Are more likely to engage in activities that improve their circumstances.
2. Work harder to develop knowledge, skills and abilities.
3. Are more inquisitive and analytical in evaluating outcomes.
4. Are more focused on achievement.

5. Tend to work harder and persevere longer.
6. Learn more from their experiences, which they then apply to future situations.

This does not mean that you can have total control. Things will happen to you over which you have no control, but you always have control of how you chose to respond to those factors. Whenever tempted to think that some person or something is "ruining your life," look in the mirror. It is almost always you doing the ruining. Playing the "victim" is a disastrous way to go through life.

Recognize that you always have a choice and that choosing not to choose is a choice in itself. Developing your decision-making and problem-solving skills enhances your control. Don't let circumstances and other people control your life.

E. Change

Change is not a four letter word! Embrace, don't attempt to avoid, positive change. Some contend that resistance to change is human nature. That is a cop-out. Change almost always involves effort. Some fear that change will mean they will lose control. Reluctance to make the effort, and fear are what generate resistance to change. To accomplish worthwhile results, you have to invest personal effort, overcome your own fears, and help others do the same.

Everything in life changes. Everything! Change is another word for evolution. *How* we evolve is our choice. *That* we evolve is not. Life is a process of continuous change. The world is constantly changing. If we don't change, we lose touch with reality. Learning changes (expands, alters) our minds. Change is how we grow. The sum total of human knowledge is doubling roughly every ten years. If we don't learn to adapt to changes, we become obsolete.

Progress is impossible without change and those who cannot change their minds, cannot change anything.
- George Bernard Shaw

F. Fairness and Justice

Don't expect the world and life to be fair and just. They are not. But you can be, and should be, thus making the world and life a little more fair and just.

Fairness and justice embrace the concepts of doing what is "right," what is consistent with the benefit of those affected, what is impartial and non-discriminatory.

These terms also have subtle, and not so subtle, nuances and interpretations that can at times conflict, and cause conflicts. "Fair" to some means equal, as in everyone should be treated equally. To others it may mean that everyone should get what they deserve, as in rewards should be related to effort. Those who produce/contribute more should get more. Those who are lazy should get less. Still another perspective is that fairness means fulfilling one's responsibilities to those in society with the greatest needs, that those who have more have an obligation to give more to those who have less. How to do the fair and just thing is not always crystal clear. We must try anyway. Think about it.

The history of this country and the world is replete with injustice, especially for those who are "different." Some contend that the fact that 30% of Americans are people of color, yet 60% of the population of the nation's prisons are people of color, is an indication that the justice "system" is biased.

The Euro-American justice system is based upon principles of punishment and retribution. The underlying logic is that, because the offender has caused a victim to suffer, the offender should be made to suffer. It is an adversarial system designed to satisfy the victim's and society's desire for revenge.

Some Eastern cultures and the Indigenous People of this continent had/have a different concept for dealing with justice. The focus is upon the restoration of balance and harmony between the offended and the offender, and the offender and the community. The emphasis is on mending. The objective is to make amends and restore relationships.

In personal relationships, seeking balance and harmony and practicing the Golden Rule are more effective than seeking revenge or "getting even."

It is in no way "fair" that some are born with physical limitations/defects, that some have abundant food, while thousands of children die every day from starvation and malnutrition.

Bad things do happen to good people. The fact is, life is not fair, is not just, and our systems of justice are imperfect. In spite of all that, we should personally strive to be fair and just and to do everything we can to promote fairness and justice.

CHAPTER 9 – CONSIDER HUMANKIND'S RELATIONSHIP TO NATURE

It is critical that we understand that our relationship to nature, and the relationship of the elements of nature to each other, are all interdependent. Animals feed on plants, and in turn animals become food for other animals and for humans. Humans exhale carbon dioxide and inhale oxygen. Trees produce oxygen and use carbon dioxide. We cannot live without trees. Nature employs an elaborate process for cleansing water, without which we cannot live.

We have a real and necessary responsibility for the guardianship of nature. The earth is not just a repository of natural resources to be exploited; it is a manifestation of life.

> *The Nature vision, the gift of seeing truly, with wonder and delight into the natural world, is informed by a certain attitude of reverence and respect. It is a matter of extrasensory as well as sensory perception. In addition to the eye, it involves the intelligence, the instinct and the imagination. It is the perception not only of objects and forms but also of essences and ideals.*
>   - N. Scott Momaday – Kiowa

Environmental quality and the quality of human life are mutually dependent. Preserving nature from the destruction of human endeavors is our moral obligation to this and future generations. We have no right to destroy the planet our grandchildren and their grandchildren will inherit. We are meant to be stewards, not exploiters, of the beauty of creation and its life giving and life enhancing functions. The challenges and responsibilities for preserving nature's abundance are daunting, but doable. What is inexcusable is the rampant and wanton abuse of nature for no reason at all, other than human indifference, laziness, and sloth.

This indifference, the mindset that "it doesn't matter," is the greatest threat to the richness and beauty of our earth.

> *Man must be made conscious of his origin as a child of Nature. Brought into a right relationship with the wilderness, he would see that he was not a separate entity endowed with a divine right to subdue his fellow creatures and destroy our common heritage, but rather an integral part of a harmonious whole. He would see that his appropriation of earth's resources beyond his personal needs can only bring imbalance and beget ultimate loss and poverty for all.*
>
> \- Linnie Marsh Wolfe

Nature should be honored as the source of the plants, animals and water that sustain our lives. More than that, we must see ourselves as part of nature, not as some higher species empowered with the privilege of exploiting it. We should see ourselves, not as having "dominion" over nature, but as a part of nature, with respect and stewardship for all other parts. We should understand that humans are not above nature, but that humans require nature to make humans "whole."

> *Every human being has a sacred duty to protect the welfare of Mother Earth, from whom all life comes. In order to do this, we must recognize the enemy, the one within us. We must begin with ourselves.*
>
> \- Leon Shenandoah, Onadaga Chief

Any desecration of nature, or taking from nature more than one requires, should be viewed as stealing from our children and grandchildren, all future generations.

> *Treat the earth well: it was not given to you by your parents, it was loaned to you by your children. We do not inherit the Earth from our ancestors, we borrow it from our children.* - Ancient Native American Proverb

Nature as Teacher - Nature is a vast reservoir of knowledge to be tapped by observation and experience. Every animal, every plant, every natural event has a lesson to convey. Observe how animals and birds care for their families. Observe what a tree limb's reaction to the wind has to teach us about the need for flexibility in our lives. By understanding nature, we can better understand ourselves. Our role is to discover the rules of the universe and to learn to live in a right relationship with them. Everything that happens has a message, something to be learned. To learn from nature involves the use of all our senses. It requires that we become involved with nature and that we become constantly observant and aware. Nature has much to teach us, if we will but open our minds.

> *It remains for us to learn once again that we are a part of nature, not a transcendent species with no responsibilities to the natural world.* - Vine Deloria, Jr.

Indigenous People found meaning in their relationship to, and love for, Mother Earth and her creatures. If we care, observe and listen, we can do likewise.

PART V - STRATEGIES FOR TAKING CONTROL OF YOUR FUTURE

Selecting valid values and principles, and building a solid character, are fundamental to taking control of your life. In conjunction with these requirements, there are several specific strategies that, if diligently practiced, will enable you to take and maintain control. Effective control may require changes to both your attitudes and your actions. The first step is to decide that you will take control. Control provides power.

CHAPTER 10 - EXAMINE YOUR ATTITUDES

A. Choose to Take Control

You can choose to view yourself as a helpless <u>victim</u> of circumstances and the whims of others, or as <u>master</u> of your fate. Lots of research indicates that those who take personal responsibility for their lives are more successful and happier than those who attribute their life consequences to external forces. Every time you blame someone else, or make excuses, you give your power away. When you take full responsibility for your life, you are in control of what you can be, do, and have.

Other research indicates that increasing one's will power is the most effective tool for improving one's life. People who have better control of their actions and emotions are healthier and happier, are better able to deal with conflicts and problems, have more satisfying relationships and less stress.

> *Educate your children to self-control, to the habit of holding passion and prejudice and evil tendencies subject to an upright and reasoning will, and you will have done much to abolish misery from their future and crimes from society.* - Benjamin Franklin

Practice demonstrating willpower on small things, - eating sweets, exercising, making your bed – these practices improve your ability to deal effectively with more significant issues. Examine your weaknesses and plan how to avoid putting yourself in positions where your willpower might weaken. If you crave smoking, but want to stop, stay away from people who smoke. Decide in advance, instead of on the spur of the moment, what you will, or will not do. Think through and commit to simple, non-ambiguous rules for self-conduct. Make negative practices that you want to avoid, as inconvenient as possible. One study indicated that the personnel in an office cut their consumption of candy by 40% when they placed the containers in drawers rather than on desk tops.

Think positively about self-discipline. Think of it not as giving things up, but as gaining control, not as denying yourself, but as achieving something.

B. Choose to Be Honest, Moral, Ethical and Truthful

There is more to determining if a decision is the "right" one, than deciding that it solves the problem, resolves the issue, or maximizes personal benefit. To be "right", a decision must not only meet your objectives, but also be moral and ethical.

Morality is about how we treat people. Right decisions are those that resolve our issues, while demonstrating respect for peoples' rights and concern for peoples' needs. "Right" decisions treat people fairly and with decency.

Mark Twain advised: *Always do right. This will gratify some people and astonish the rest.*

Morality is not just abstaining from a list of things one shouldn't do. It is about doing what one should do, what is right.

> *The most important human endeavor is the striving for morality in our actions. Our inner balance, and even our very existence depends on it. Only morality in our actions can give beauty and dignity to our lives.*
> — Dr. Albert Einstein

Coach John Wooden relates that he received what proved to be valuable wisdom from his father, who taught "two sets of threes:"

> Never lie.
> Never cheat.
> Never steal.
>
> Don't whine.
> Don't complain.
> Don't make excuses.

C. Choose to Think.

> *Just think. Just be quiet and think. It will make all the difference in the world.*
> — Mr. Rogers

It is amazing, and often disastrous, how often people act impulsively, reacting emotionally, rather than thinking. People who live meaningful, effective and fulfilling lives think differently than those who don't. To accomplish anything, you have to take action, and the success of any action depends on the thoughts that initiated it. All that one achieves, or fails to achieve, is the direct result of one's thoughts.

Think about who you are. Think about who you want to be. Think about what you love. Think about what is sacred. Think about what is true. Think about what you want to learn. Think about your values and principles. Think about the fact that you will die and that experiencing this day is a gift. Think about what is important. Think about what is priceless. Think about how you wish to live your life.

Be a "critical" (not negative, but questioning) thinker. Ask: What evidence, experience, authority supports this statement, contention, theory? Is the evidence verifiable and complete? Are the premises valid? Are my intentions honorable, and right for all concerned?

Effective thinking is seeking the whole picture, looking for relationships, looking for patterns rather than pieces. To make effective decisions about how to live, it is critical to develop the ability to reason accurately and independently, rather than accepting answers based upon authority or tradition. We become what we think. To get control of your life, you have to think, and control what you think.

> *Self-control is strength; Right thought is mastery;*
> *Calmness is power.*   - James Allen

Clear thinking involves effectively gathering, accessing and integrating the multiple messages coming at you from the reality around you and within you. The characteristic that makes us uniquely human is the ability of our minds to examine their own processes, to think about thinking. We can, and should, mentally examine: How did I reach that conclusion? Was my conclusion influenced by my prejudices? Is my conclusion logical or does it reflect the way I want things to be? What are my goals and objectives? Will this decision enable or impede my goals? What kind of person do I want to be? Are my actions consistent with who I want to be?

Thinking is, of course, only the first step. The right thoughts are critical, for they drive action, but what really matters is what you do. The objective is to produce the right results. The quality of results are almost always determined by the strength and quality of the thinking expended in achieving them.

Words are powerful. Think before you speak. Consider the three "gatekeepers" that the Buddha advised we consider before speaking:

> *Is what I am about to say true?*
> *Is what I am about to say necessary?*
> *Will what I am about to say do no harm?*

Thinking clearly takes commitment, effort and practice, but the benefits are well worth the effort. Your ability to think, and to think about thinking, is a tremendous gift. Use it or lose it.

1. Think About Your Current Reality.
    a. Am I a good daughter/son?
    b. Am I a good brother/sister?
    c. Am I a good friend?
    d. Am I a good student?
    e. Do I always act morally, ethically?
    f. Am I living up to my potential? Could I be a better person?

If you are dissatisfied with the answers to any of these questions, think about how you might change your thoughts and behavior to align with who you want to be.

Thoughts determine actions. Actions have consequences.

2. Think About Outcomes.

Determine what you really want and then about how to get there.

Consider: How might my life be better if I change my priorities?

    a. How might my life be better if I change how I spend my time?
    b. How might my life be better if I develop _____ (a certain skill or ability)?
    c. How might my life be better if I treated _____ (someone) differently?
    d. How might my life be better if I learned _____?
    e. How might my life be better if I gave up _____?

D. Choose to Accept Responsibility

No matter how good or bad your decisions, you are responsible for the consequences. You are responsible for your thoughts, beliefs, values, words, choices and actions. You are responsible for how you treat other people, for keeping your promises, for your life and personal well-being. Blaming others or finding excuses does not change that reality. Recognizing and accepting this responsibility will enable you to make better decisions.

These three words can change your life: "I am responsible." It is only when you accept complete responsibility that you take the giant step from childhood to adulthood. When you focus on what you can do, and how you should act, you gain power. Accepting responsibility is the key to personal effectiveness in every sphere of life.

> **Avoid Lame Excuses**
>
> Explanation of a driver stopped by a policeman for speeding:
>
> "I know I was going too fast, but I was trying to blow the snow off my windshield so I could see where I was going."

Being responsible requires self-discipline and effective time management. It means being conscientious, mindful, accountable and dependable. Be particularly conscious of what you say, for words can wound deeper than a knife. Accept that you have control. If you don't do <u>something</u>, nothing is going to get better. Choose not to be a victim. Don't, as many do, blame your circumstances on someone else's actions, or on the "system," or the "breaks." Accepting responsibility is the first step to finding solutions.

Be pro-active. Avoid the mindset of "Why doesn't someone do something?" Instead ask, "What should I do?" Then do something.

The respect and trust of persons who you respect and trust are valuable assets. You earn that respect and trust by being competent and accountable, and by accepting responsibility for your actions.

Take responsibility for learning to make better decisions. Make the best decision you know how to make and take responsibility for the consequences.

Accepting responsibility should not be viewed as a burden. It is a privilege and an honor to take ownership of your actions. It creates freedom and control. It gives meaning to life.

E. Choose To Be Conscientious

Literally, being conscientious means following one's conscience, doing what is right. Developing a sound value system and living those values are important.

Conscientiousness also means more. Being conscientious means being dependable, doing what you say you will do, and being there for others, demonstrating that others can count on you. Being conscientious means being aware of, and responsive to, the needs of others.

F. Choose to Be Tenacious/Persistent

Not all of your choices will turn out to be good ones. Not everything you try will succeed. YOU WILL FAIL! (That's a good thing). It's not just OK, it's essential.

Those who excel at whatever they do have learned to learn from failures. The excellent fail more often than the mediocre, because they attempt more. They succeed because they have failed more and learned from their failures.

> *I do not think that there is any other quality so essential to success of any kind as the quality of perseverance. It overcomes almost everything.*
> - John D. Rockefeller

It is only from the experience of challenging ourselves that we learn and grow, and we often mature and learn more from our failures than from our successes. When we put ourselves on the line, when we fall down and get up again, we become stronger and more resilient. You will fail. It will never be particularly pleasant. The key is to learn from the process. Consciously reflect on the process and ask: "What did I learn that will be of benefit for my next experience?"

In 1910, President Theodore Roosevelt included these remarks in a speech:

> *It is not the critic who counts; nor the man who points out how the strong man stumbles, or where the doer of deeds could have done them better. The credit belongs to the man who is actually in the arena, whose face is marred by dust, sweat and blood; who strives valiantly; who errs, who comes up short again and again, because there is no effort without error and shortcoming; but he who actually strives to do the deeds; who knows great enthusiasms, the great devotions, who spends himself in a worthy cause; who at the best, knows in the end the triumph of high achievement and who at the worst, if he fails while daring greatly, knows that his place shall never be with those cold and timid souls who know neither victory or defeat.*

Mr. Roosevelt made a valid observation.

Failure does not have to be an end point. If a goal is worthy, and an approach did not work, and if you learned from the experience, trying again with a modified approach is a viable option. Success depends on staying power.

PRESS ON

> *Nothing in the world can take the place of persistence.*
>
> *Talent will not; nothing is more common than unsuccessful people with talent. Genius will not; unrewarded genius is almost a proverb.*
>
> *Education alone will not; the world is full of educated derelicts. Persistence and determination alone are omnipotent.*
>
>   - Anonymous

I have had the above quote on my wall for years and found its truth apparent in multiple instances. Here are three different perspectives on failing and persevering:

> *A failure is not always a mistake. It may simply be the best one can do under the circumstances. The real mistake is to stop trying.* - B. F. Skinner

> *Through perseverance many people win success out of what seemed destined to be certain failure.*
> - Benjamin Disraeli

> *How much you can learn when you fail determines how far you will go in achieving your goals.* - Roy Bennett

You do not need to be perfect, nor measure your worth by the standards of others. You do not have to make overnight giant strides in productivity. You should just strive to become a little better every day. You can take pride and comfort in whatever you do if you understand that you have done your best.

> *The real contest, of course, is striving to reach your personal best, and that is totally under your control. When you achieve that, you have achieved success. Period! You are a winner and only you fully know if you have won.*
> - John Wooden.

G. Choose To Be Adaptable

Be willing to change and choose to manage change.

> *The world as we have created it is a result of our thinking. It cannot be changed without changing our thinking.*
> - Albert Einstein

We are constantly making decisions, big and small. These choices are about what we will change and how. Each night, when we go to bed, we are different from the person we were when we got up. Our challenge is to make the change positive and productive.

> *Incredible change happens in your life when you decide to take control of what you do have power over, instead of craving control over what you don't.* - Steve Maraboli

We are all involved in many roles: sibling, son, daughter, student, employee, group member, friend, etc. etc. Striving to become better at fulfilling those roles is a worthwhile objective. It enriches our lives and the lives of others. Becoming stagnant or failing to fulfil our responsibilities in these roles means falling short of our potential.

This is as true for individuals and for organizations. If you want your life to be more fulfilling, you must change mindset and behavior. Resisting change is self-limiting. It shuts off possibilities and opportunities.

The attitude that we are helpless victims of our history or our circumstances is a cop out. We all have the ability to change.

> *For what it's worth: it's never too late or, too early to be whoever you want to be. There's no time limit, stop whenever you want. You can change or stay the same, there are no rules to this thing. We can make the best or the worst of it. I hope you make the best of it. And I hope you see things that startle you. I hope you feel things you never felt before. I hope you meet people with a different point of view. I hope you live a life you're proud of. If you find that you're not, I hope you have the courage to start all over again.* - Eric Roth

Your focus should be on how to make changes that make you, your relationships, and the world better, not worse. Resolving and striving to become a better person and to help improve the lives of others are worthwhile goals, and increase the probability that inevitable changes will be positive.

Improvement will not happen without change.

CHANGE – don't fight it, promote it!

> *Be the change that you wish to see in the world.*
> \- Mahatma Gandhi

H. Choose to Be Willing to Work

How we view work has a lot to do with our comfort level with life. If we view work as punishment, drudgery, a necessary evil, the price we have to pay to make a living, chances are we will: not do it very well, will derive little satisfaction from it, and will find our lives full of stress. If we don't do it very well, it is not likely to impress those to whom we are responsible. That will inevitably lead to more stress.

If you view work as a challenge, an opportunity to learn, grow, and demonstrate your abilities to do "good" work, it can be a source of pride, self-esteem and satisfaction. No matter the level of responsibility, even if it is sweeping streets, doing well <u>what</u> you do is important; emotionally, psychologically and monetarily.

Work at developing a positive perspective about work.

> *Opportunity is missed by most people because it is dressed in overalls and looks like work.*
> \- Thomas Edison

I. Choose To Be Mindful

There are two elements to mindfulness: being <u>aware</u>, being conscious of what is going on around us, and <u>focus,</u> having the ability to concentrate on one thing, to give that one thing our undivided attention, so we can deal with it most effectively.

> *The mind is just like a muscle – the more you exercise it, the stronger it gets and the more it can expand.*
> \- Idowu Koyenikan

Awareness. You have probably observed people who seemed oblivious to what was going on around them, who were out of touch with reality. This "condition" is hardly conducive to making good choices. Circumstances matter, conditions matter, context matters, how the world really works (reality) matters. Being aware means being conscious of everything that affects your: interests, actions, goals, objectives, and values. Being aware means being willing to confront reality, whether pleasant or unpleasant. Being aware means being conscious of, and respectful of, facts, reality, and truth. To learn to make better decisions, you need to learn to be aware.

Awareness is a choice, and also a skill that can be developed. Awareness means being awake to the here and now. It is about being keenly observant of what is going on and why, of what conditions exist, and why.

Understand that we control awareness like a dimmer switch on an electric light. We can willfully increase or decrease our sensitivity to our surroundings and what is going on. It is not practical to be 100% aware, 100% of the time. Your level of awareness is a choice. Context, the nature and importance of what is present, and what is going on should determine where you set your "awareness switch". To operate effectively, you need to determine which things can be left on "automatic," and which things warrant your full attention.

> *Mindfulness means being awake. It means knowing what you are doing.* - Jon Kabat-Zinn

Unfortunately many of us make important, sometimes life changing, decisions with little or no awareness of how those choices will change the shape and direction of our lives. We commit to actions without considering the consequences. Awareness is critical to effective decision-making.

Focus. Mindfulness is our basic tool for adapting to, and successfully coping with, reality.

Our minds naturally have a tendency to jump around from one subject to another like a monkey jumping from one branch to the next. Controlling what Buddhists refer to as our "monkey minds," is essential to rational thought and effective decision-making. To "bind the monkey," we must understand our minds, our feelings and perceptions, and learn to focus on one thing at a time.

> *Concentration is a cornerstone of mindfulness practice. Your mindfulness will only be as robust as the capacity of your mind to be calm and stable. Without calmness, the mirror of mindfulness will have an agitated and choppy surface and will not be able to reflect things with any accuracy.* - Jon Kabat-Zinn

Fortunately, you can learn to be mindful. Like any life skill, it takes time and effort. The first, and essential, step is to decide that you <u>want</u> to learn to be mindful.

To make better decisions, to make improvements, the starting point is awareness. Pay attention. Be "present." When walking a path in the woods, notice the leaves, the weeds, the bark on the trees, the wildlife, the patterns created by sunlight sifting through the canopy. When walking a city street, notice the varying architecture of buildings, the cars passing, and especially the people. When participating in a meeting, observe: not only the content, but the ongoing "process." What does the body language of participants indicate? What role is authority playing in the meeting? What "hidden agendas" are being served? Be observant.

When dealing with a problem or issue, concentrate on concentrating. When your mind strays, gently bring it back to the subject at hand. Focus on your written definition of the issue. It will help you concentrate. Jot down your thoughts. It will help you concentrate.

The "Law of Cause and Effect" asserts that for every effect there is a cause. When you observe an effect, think about, and identify, the possible causes. Many practitioners, myself included, contend that you can train your mind to be more mindful through the practice of meditation. Thich Nhat Hanh defines mindfulness as "keeping one's consciousness alive to the present reality." When we practice mindfulness in order to build up concentration, mindfulness is like a seed. Properly tended, it grows. Mindfulness frees us of forgetfulness and dispersion, and makes it possible to live fully each moment of life. To learn more about improving mindfulness through meditation, read: *The Miracle of Mindfulness*, by Thich Nhat Hanh.

> *Training your mind to be in the present moment is the #1 key to making healthier choices.*
> - Susan Albers

J. Choose to be Grateful.

Count your blessings instead of your woes. Focusing on what you have, and expressing thankfulness, helps you cope with the desire to have what you would like to have, but don't have. Thinking about, and appreciating, the good that has happened to you helps you deal with the not so good that inevitably happens. Contemplating your achievements and their contributions to your life, helps you deal with adversities.

CHAPTER 11 – MAKE THINGS HAPPEN

A positive attitude is important, but it is not enough. If you really want to improve your life, you must take action. That takes self-discipline, willpower, and self-control. We tend to attempt to avoid problems and emotional pain. Avoidance doesn't cut it. You need to view pain and problems as challenges and understand that, although it may not be easy, you have the ability to deal with them.

Understand that your past does not determine your future. Nelson Gant spent his early years as a slave. He became a prosperous man, and a contributing, respected citizen. Gabby Thomas grew up in poverty. She earned a master's degree, a responsible career, and three gold medals in the 2024 Olympics. Stephen Hawking, an almost totally paralyzed physicist, made significant contributions to our knowledge, in spite of severe physical handicaps.

There are things YOU can DO to take control.

A. Build Positive Relationships

Relationships are key. Focus on building positive relationships with persons worthy of your trust. Treat People as You Want to Be Treated.

> *People will forget what you said, people will forget what you did, but people will never forget how you made them feel.*
> - Bonnie Jean Wasmund

B. Develop Useful Life Skills.

There are certain life skills that are especially useful for helping you control your future.

1. Learn to Learn.

Be a learner. Learning one new thing does not make you an expert, but a commitment to lifelong learning can change your life. No matter how it turns out, every experience has something to teach you. Reflect on your major decisions, and the consequences. In anticipation of an experience, contemplate: "What should I learn from this?" After each experience, ask yourself: "What did I learn from that?"

Develop a learning mindset. It is a skill that can be developed and improved. Develop an interest in acquiring knowledge. Ask lots of questions; to yourself and to others. Learning is more than schooling. It is a state of mind, a willingness to consciously look at the world and life with an endless sense of curiosity and wonder. View learning as something delightful. Seek mentors and teachers who can help with the process.

With a learning mindset, setbacks are not failures. They become data that can be framed into opportunities to learn, and improve. The first time a child touches a hot stove, the child learns something. That information is stored in a data bank and is used for shaping future decisions. Every experience has that potential, but the process is much more effective if you make a conscious effort to learn from your experiences.

One of the ultimate purposes of life is to learn. Learning gives life meaning and helps us understand life's meaning. Learning enables more effective decision-making. Life is a school, complete with tests. The tests can help us learn what we need to learn.

Deliberately expose yourself to new experiences, ideas, information and opinions. Consciously and continuously strive to be more aware, more knowledgeable and more understanding of everything that is relevant to you. Learning can be fun, not a chore, if you **decide** it is fun. Life will be more interesting and exciting if you are constantly learning.

Learn from experience. Doing the same thing over and over and expecting different results is one of the definitions of insanity. Doing *more* of what doesn't work, does not work. Focus on what does work, and do more of that. When traditional solutions don't work, create new approaches to try.

Writing can help you learn. In high school and college, I strongly disliked writing courses. They seemed like work. In graduate school, I was forced to write more and got better at it, but still didn't particularly like it. As a management consultant, I had to write reports often. Since then, I have learned the wisdom of the following observation:

> *Learning to write is learning to think. You don't know anything clearly unless you can state it in writing.*
> *- S. I. Hayakawa*

Learn from mistakes. We all make them. Don't let mistakes discourage you. They are opportunities to learn. Admit them. Examine the "why." Reflect on the lessons learned. Keep an open mind. Make adjustments. Try again, or try something else. The critical thing is to learn from the experience.

The world, life, is constantly changing. To cope, to thrive, we must adapt. To remain adaptive, we must commit to a life of continuous learning.

> *The capacity to learn is a **gift**.*
> *The ability to learn is a **skill**.*
> *The willingness to learn is a **choice**.*
> *- Brian Herbert*

2. Hone Your Curiosity

Consciously strive to develop a healthy curiosity. It is a trait that can be developed, and can broaden knowledge and perspectives. Try new experiences. Explore new places. Ask "why" questions. Curiosity generates energy, gets us involved in life, facilitates learning, uncovers opportunities and adds to the quality of our lives. A prime driver of learning is the search for answers to life's questions, the questions that engage our minds, reflect our interests, and influence the direction and quality of our lives. Curiosity can be developed if you have the desire and the discipline to work at it. Michael Gelb, in his book; *How to Think Like Leonardo da Vinci,* suggests that we:

a) Keep a journal
b) Jot down ideas, impressions and observations as they occur.
c) In your notebook, make a list of 100 questions that you think are important.
d) Review your list and choose the 10 that seem most significant.
e) Rank the 10 in order of importance to you.
f) Set aside a time to contemplate the first question on your list.
g) Explore the alternatives. Look for themes and relationships. Concentrate, until you are satisfied that you have a valid answer.
h) Repeat with each question.

Develop an insatiable curiosity. The continuous quest for learning is a powerful force.

3. Learn to Listen.

The most useful skill to learn for dealing effectively with people is the skill of listening, really LISTENING. Real listening can't happen unless you have a sincere desire to understand what you're hearing, and that's not an easy task to manage. Real listening requires intention, concentration and effort. Listening may seem like giving up power, because you are not in control of the conversation. In fact, it enhances the probability of effective outcomes. "When you stop preaching and really listen, here's what happens:" (from *The 7 Habits of Highly Effective People, by Stephen Covey*)

> **Check the Meaning of Vague Messages**
>
> My new girlfriend left a note on the windshield of my new Porsche. It read: "This isn't working." I got very nervous. I was relieved when I started the car and found that it was working fine.

a) People are more willing to trust you. If you don't have people's trust, you will never be able to influence them.

b) You acquire useful information, which makes it much easier to find solutions.

c) You gain insight into other people's perceptions and what it will take to make a solution acceptable to them.

d) You begin to see other people as individuals – and maybe even allies. Together, you can move from I/they to "us."

e) You can develop solutions that other people are willing to accept and even support. When people contribute to the solutions, become co-owners, they are more likely to commit and follow through.

f) When people feel heard, they are more willing to listen. If people do not feel that you "get" them, they are not inclined to expend the effort to listen to, and understand you.

This is not to say that listening guarantees a favorable outcome every time, but failure to listen usually guarantees that the outcome will not be optimal, and it may create a complete failure.

In *The 7 Habits,* Covey refers to this skill as "empathic listening," and urges us to "Seek First to Understand and Then to be Understood."

He indicates that: "next to physical survival, the greatest need of a human being is to be understood, to be affirmed, to be validated, to be appreciated. Listening with empathy to another person provides that person with psychological 'air.' Once that need is met, you can move on to problem-solving or influencing." If that need is not first met, the person will be too preoccupied with "gasping for air" to appreciate the wisdom of your solutions. They are not likely to listen to you until you have listened to them.

LEARN to listen. It's amazing what you will LEARN. LISTEN to learn, not to frame your reply. Take time to listen, to others and to the still, small voice inside. Your unconscious often has something useful to convey.

4. Learn to Use Time Wisely.

    Time is our most precious resource. Time decisions are among the most important you make. You make decisions all day, every day, about how you are going to use your time. You may ask yourself: "What am I going to do: today?, this morning?, for the next hour?, for the next 10 minutes?" Or, you may not consciously ask these critical questions and just let time slide. Remember that a decision not to decide is still a decision. How you answer these questions affects the quality of your life. When you are asked to do something, or decide to do something, that requires a commitment of your time, understand that the commitment represents a piece of your life. Recognize that your time = your life. Ask yourself if playing time-devouring video games or watching mind-numbing TV is really how you want to spend your <u>life</u>.

> *Dost thou love life? Then do not squander time, for that's the stuff life is made of.*
> - Benjamin Franklin.

When thinking about time, think not about saving time, but "making time" for things that matter. Make a list of the distractions, (junk emails, texts, social media, streaming, etc.) that steal your time every day. Identify ways to eliminate those thieves from your agenda. At the end of each day, or the first thing in the morning, select two or three significant tasks for the day. Write them down. Schedule one or more times to work on those tasks. Lock out the distractions. Focus during those times. Get the tasks done.

This is not to imply that we should work all the time. Everyone needs to spend time having fun, learning, exercising, spiritually recharging and just relaxing. Just be conscious of the importance of time, and be <u>intentional</u> about how you use it.

> *This time, like all times, is a very good one, if we but know how to use it.*   - Ralph Waldo Emerson

C. Read

Experiences enhance our ability to make effective decisions and cope with challenges. They enrich our lives. You should seek out and take advantage of opportunities to create and embrace positive personal experiences. But, there is a practical limit to what you can personally experience. There is simply not enough time to learn, through experiences, what you need to learn. There is a much broader scope of wisdom available, if you include learning from what others have written about their experiences and what they learned from them, whether fact or fiction. It's a cliché, but true, that those who don't read are no better off than those who can't.

> *The more you read, the more things you will know. The more you know, the more places you'll go.*
> *- Dr. Suess*

There is much to read and you must be selective. There is a lot of junk written. To develop wisdom it is important to reflect on the thoughts of the world's wisest thinkers.

> *Employ your time in improving yourself by other men's writings so that you shall come easily by what others labored hard for. - Socrates*

Reading can take us to worlds we will never see and helps us understand and learn from people of cultures we will never encounter. It enables us to travel instantly through distance and time, to understand our origins, our heritage and the lessons of history. It helps us understand how the world works and why people act the way they do. It stretches our minds and helps us see the world in new ways. It increases our sensitivity to people and to nature. Reading prepares us for life and changes lives. Reading can help us understand how to be better human beings.

> *No matter how busy you think you are, you must find time for reading, or surrender yourself to self-chosen ignorance.*
> *- Atwood H. Townsend*

> *Reading is everything. Reading makes me feel like I've accomplished something, learned something, become a better person. Reading makes me smarter. Reading gives*

me something to talk about. Reading is escape, and the opposite of escape. It's a way to make contact with reality. It's a way of making contact with someone else's imagination. Reading is grist. Reading is bliss.
- Nora Ephron

Reading has had such a positive influence in my life that I cannot resist urging you to read, selectively but extensively. I consider writing and reading one of humankind's greatest achievements. A suggested starter list of books is included in Appendix P. Try some of them.

What an astonishing thing a book is. It's a flat object made from a tree with flexible parts on which are imprinted lots of funny dark squiggles. But one glance at it and you're inside the mind of another person, maybe somebody dead for thousands of years.

Across the millennia, an author is speaking clearly and silently inside your head, directly to you. Writing is perhaps the greatest of human inventions, binding together people who never knew each other, people of distant epochs. Books break the shackles of time. A book is proof that humans are capable of working magic.
- Carl Sagan

D. Exercise Self-Control

Demonstrating self-control involves choosing thoughtful, rational responses to outside stimuli, which are consistent with ones values and goals. It is the process of avoiding compulsive, self-destructive reactions to temptations, threats, addictions or provocations. Permitting negative emotions to influence decisions can have devastating effects. Self-control is about being the master of one's life rather than the slave to one's emotions. It is not about taking all the fun out of life. It is about making intelligent choices. Self-control is a combination of will, commitment, courage, and taking responsibility for one's actions. It is also a concept of free will and choice. You have to choose to exercise it.

> *If you are not in control of your thoughts, then you are not in control of yourself. Without self-control, you have no real power, regardless of whatever else you accomplish. If you are not aware of the thoughts that you are thinking, then you are a rider with no reins, with no power over where you are going. You cannot control what you are not aware of. Awareness must come first.*
> - Thomas M. Steiner

Impulsive, irrational behaviors can result in poor decisions that: are harmful to personal heath and well- being, can impair personal effectiveness, and can damage relationships.

Developing self-control involves awareness, the understanding that we can choose our emotions and thoughts, and the identification of our personal "hot buttons," those stimuli that typically set off automatic, personal and/or relationship damaging, emotional responses.

To establish control:

1. Identify personal issues/instances over which you wish to exert more effective control.
2. Identify the damaging, typical reactions to which you are prone and the emotions that drive them.
3. Make a decision to develop more effective responses.
4. Tell yourself: "I am in control of my thoughts, emotions and reactions, I am in charge of my behavior."
5. Visualize how you would like to calmly and rationally deal with the issue.

6. Recognize the volatile issue when they come up and <u>practice</u> your planned responses.

The good news is that, like a muscle, self-control gets stronger with regular exercise. The important thing is to practice overriding damaging, habitual ways of doing things, and exerting deliberate control over your actions.

Respond intelligently, even to unintelligent treatment.
— Lao-Tzu

Never respond to an angry person with a fiery comeback, even if he deserves it. Don't allow his anger to become your anger.
— Bohdi Sanders

We can control our thoughts. That's a powerful concept that can make a difference in life. Practice it.

E. Seek Justice, Fairness and Peace

Treat others fairly and demonstrate the courage to oppose injustice. Injustice often prevails, not because everyone approves, but because few have the courage to openly disapprove. Promote peace by learning to reconcile differences. Advocate for diversity and inclusion. Support efforts to find non-violent resolution to local, national and international conflicts. Become involved in positive efforts to support justice and peace.

F. Control the Way You Talk to Yourself

We all talk to ourselves constantly. Make the tone of those conversations positive, not critical or negative. Don't beat yourself up for mistakes or shortcomings. Don't delude yourself about reality, but focus on accomplishments and successes. Understand your feelings, but focus on your behavior. You feel the way you feel because of what you do. If you want to change how you feel, change what you are doing. Anger and fear are major impediments to rational decision-making. Talk with yourself about your anger and fears. Ask yourself how you would like to act if you were not angry or afraid.

Studies show that positive self-talk has a positive benefit for maintaining self-control.

G. Choose a Satisfying Vocation

Choose a vocation carefully. One of the most critical life decisions we make is the choice of the kind of work we do. Work helps define who we are, because that is where we spend a lot of our time. Most of us spend 35% or more of our waking hours at some type of occupation, and many spend far more time thinking or worrying about that activity. The wrong choice can lead to what Thoreau described as a life of "quiet desperation." In some cases, the desperation can become more than "quiet."

Choose a vocation, not a job. The word vocation comes from the Latin word for "calling." Your life will be more pleasant if you can work at something you feel "called" to do. Consciously search for a vocation that interests you, appeals to you, and one from which you can derive satisfaction, not just a living. Research jobs to learn what is actually involved.

We talked earlier about the importance of personal values. A critical criterion for choosing an employment opportunity is to make certain that the values of your employer match your own. If you believe in the mission of the organization, it is much easier to get motivated to do well at your job and derive satisfaction from doing it.

There are two types of values derived from work: extrinsic and intrinsic. Extrinsic values, pay and benefits, are necessary, but not sufficient. Focusing only on extrinsic values will lead to unhealthiness and unhappiness. You need enough extrinsic compensation to be comfortable, but it is the intrinsic rewards that determine if you are satisfied and happy. Apply two basic criteria to your job choice: (1) Will it be satisfying? Will doing it well make you feel good? (2) Will it serve others? Does the work have intrinsic worth? Will the world be a better place because you do your job well?

First, know yourself. Understand your abilities, interests, and what you don't like. There are multiple "tests" available that attempt to match personal interests and abilities to vocations. Try them.

When considering what you want to do for the remainder of your working life, the following process may prove useful:

a. List your strengths and weaknesses.
b. List your likes and don't likes.
c. List your vocational goals and ambitions.
d. Select the income level you would like to achieve at various points in your career.
e. Make a list of the occupations the fit with your self-assessment.
f. Gather information about those occupations.
g. Narrow your list to the few that most interest you.
h. Conduct further research. Talk to people in those occupations. Identify the educational and other requirements. Create opportunities to actually try the work to see if it fits.
i. Check the alternatives against your values, goals and objectives.
j. Make a choice.
k. Develop a plan to make your choice happen.
l. Look for an opportunity to work hard at something worth doing, and something you enjoy doing. The benefit of the

right vocation is not how much it pays, but what it helps you become.

Make sure that your choice is yours, not what someone thinks you should do, or what is available or convenient. If your choice does not work out, don't be afraid to change. Repeat the process and try something else.

H. Demonstrate Respect and Reverence for Nature

Modern environmental problems have become so serious that they constitute a global crisis. We are destroying our home. Native Americans lived comfortably with nature for thousands of years. Conservation was a basic value of their culture. White cultures strive to <u>control</u> nature. The Indigenous People focused on <u>cooperating</u> with nature.

Their concepts of their responsibilities to nature included:

    a. Continually giving thanks for the life-giving power of the sun, for the earth and the water and food the earth provides.
    b. Never taking more than one needs.
    c. Giving thanks for what we do take.
    d. Replenishing what is taken.
    e. Doing as little damage as possible.
    f. Taking time to appreciate the beauty of the earth.

We could benefit greatly by adopting these attitudes.

Nature is important. All nature, including humankind, is interconnected and interdependent. Experience it. Pay attention to it. Nurture it and preserve it. Our future and that of our children and grandchildren depend on it.

In *Voices In the Stones*, Kent Nerburn quotes a Native American elder who said:

> *Nature has rules. Nature has laws. You think that you can ignore the rules or, if you don't like them, you can change them. But Mother Earth doesn't change the rules. When you can count the animals, you're getting near the end of your chances. We can count the eagles. We can count the buffalo. I've heard that in India and Africa they can count the tigers and the elephants. That's Mother Earth crying out. She's giving us a warning and She's begging for her life. And here's what your people don't ever seem to learn, there's going to become a day when things can't be fixed. And you know what? It's going to be a day just like today.*

I. Establish Boundaries

Boundaries define the limits of what is you and what is not you. Boundaries define the limits beyond which you will not go. We hear a lot about "will power." Equally as important is "wont power." Develop your personal list of "Wonts," and stick to them.

J. Organize for Effectiveness

Many people use "to do" lists to help them remember, keep their thoughts organized, and use their time more effectively. I prefer a to-do list with a wrinkle: I find it effective to divide a to do list into four quadrants.

TO DO LIST

	Urgent	Not Urgent
Important		
Not Important		

This approach encourages you to focus on those tasks, (the ones in the top left quadrant), that are likely to produce the most benefit. The format is a variation of what Stephen Covey called a "Time Management Matrix" in *The 7 Habits of Highly Effective People*, and what is sometimes referred to as the "Eisenhower Box," because it was used by former President and Five Star General Dwight D. Eisenhower. I suggest keeping a 3" X 5" card in your pocket or purse, with the left two quadrants on one side of the card, the right two quadrants on the other side, and that you prepare a new card daily.

Many find journaling useful and recommend it as a regular practice. I agree. I find it effective to have a simple three ring notebook handy. I suggest tabs with the following categories:

1. JOURNAL – lots of blank pages for frequent recording of thoughts, events, insights.
2. VALUES, PRINCIPLES, CHARACTER – list of those you wish to incorporate.
3. MISSION, GOALS, OBJECTIVES – your personal statements.
4. MAJOR PROJECTS – your bucket list of things you wish to accomplish.
5. DECISION REVIEW LOG – as described above, and shown in Appendix O.

K. Seek Wisdom

Everyone has something to offer. You should focus, not on what you can get or accumulate, but on what you can be and what you can give. The beginning of wisdom is determining what that should be, who you are, and how you want to live. With wisdom comes an understanding of, and appreciation of, meaning.

> *We are here to do.*
> *And through doing to learn;*
> *and through learning to know;*
> *and through knowing to experience wonder;*
> *and through wonder to attain wisdom;*
> *and through wisdom to find simplicity;*
> *and through simplicity to give attention;*

*and through attention
to see what needs to be done.*
- Ben Hei, Jewish Sage

An important element of wisdom is to understand that, despite our differences, humans are much more alike than different. We all live and we all die. We all hurt. We all laugh. We all cry. We all have problems. We all suffer losses. We all grieve. We all want to be loved. We all want to be respected. We all want to be treated fairly. We are all related. We are all in this together.

Please read and think about the story in Case Study 12, "Overcoming Adversities," at the end of this chapter.

CASE STUDY 12 - OVERCOMING ADVERSITIES

Brad's early years were more traumatic than most. He never knew who his father was, and his mother was a heroin addict. His early memories were of digging through trash barrels to find food, of violent men who showed up at all hours at the apartment he shared with his mother, and of his mother disappearing for days at a time.

When I talked with one of his elementary school teachers about Brad, she said it was the saddest situations she had ever seen. She related that three times during the nine months he was in her class, she had referred Brad to Children's Services. They would keep him for a few days and then turn him over to a relative. Shortly thereafter, the relative would take him back to his mother.

In spite of his difficulties, Brad did fairly well in elementary school. His report cards indicated that he was intelligent, a fast learner, a responsible student, and a good friend to his classmates. In middle school, he started to go off track. The report card comments changed to: "Brad needs to focus in class, Brad misses assignments and is in danger of failing, Brad often loses his temper in class, Brad seems to be bright, but lacks motivation." By the end of middle school, he had racked up a serious array of discipline infractions; from alcohol possession, to defiance, to fighting, for which he spent significant time on suspension. His GPA dropped to 1.25 and he almost never completed assignments.

Brad did not get off to a good start at our high school. Early in his freshman year, he got into a serious fight with another student. For this rules violation, he was expelled, and spent the rest of his first year of high school in a school for "special" students. There, he met a teacher, Mr. Johnson, who figured out that, beneath all the anger, there was a person of intelligence, compassion and integrity.

With Mr. Johnson's help, Brad turned his life around. Mr. Johnson listened, counseled, believed in him, and cared about him. Brad's grades improved and his behavior problems disappeared.

During the summer, I was faced with a tough decision. As principal of the high school, I had to decide if Brad should be re-admitted. I had his files, which showed dramatic improvements in grades and behavior, and an appeal letter from Mr. Johnson, urging that I give Brad another chance. I had reservations about whether Brad could keep his act together in a large public high school, especially without the daily support of Mr. Johnson.

I met with Brad, and concluded that he should have the chance to prove himself. I'm thankful that I made that decision. He seemed very appreciative of the chance and we developed a close relationship, which continues to this day. I enlisted the help of a couple of the young men who were among the leaders in our school, and asked that they help Brad get acclimated. The three became friends.

Brad worked hard and graduated from high school. His GPA for the last three years was 3.3. He played sports, and was elected to the homecoming court his senior year. At graduation from our school, the senior class elects one senior to give a motivational speech at commencement. Brad was the unanimous choice.

He asked me to help him with his speech. As he struggled with the details, I got choked up. He wrapped his 6' 3" frame around my shoulders and said:

"I'm ok that all that stuff happened to me. I wouldn't be who I am today if I hadn't lived through it. It made me stronger."

Brad helped me realize that it is through our struggles, not our successes, that we grow. Brad had learned to accept his past, to make peace with it and to learn from it.

Four years later, I attended Brad's college graduation. When he told me that day that he had decided to become a teacher, it was the highlight of my educational career.

What were the factors that helped Brad turn his life around?

Do we ever really know why other people act the way they do?

Have you ever known anyone whose negative behaviors were hard to understand?

How might you help someone whose negative behavior may indicate that they are struggling with problems?

PART VI - PULL IT ALL TOGETHER

Clarifying values, developing principles and building character will make you a better you. Improving your decision making skills will make you more effective. To become the person you want to be, it is very helpful to pull together, into a plan, your values, principles, the character traits to which you aspire, along with your goals, objectives, and strategies.

CHAPTER 12 - DEVELOP A PURPOSE

Selecting a purpose gives your life a reason for being and a focus. Your purpose should include a commitment to do something you consider meaningful and beneficial for humankind.

> *It's not enough to have lived. We should be determined to live for something.*
> *- Dr. Leo Buscaglia*

It starts with identifying the right path to walk, the right way to live, and then selecting a purpose to which you are willing to devote your efforts. Ask: What does the world need that I would feel good about providing? If you have a worthy purpose, a plan, and the persistence to pursue that purpose, it makes life worth living.

> *They say there are two important days in your life: the day you were born and the day you find out why you were born.*
> *- Carl Townsend*

Having a purpose does not guarantee that life will be easy. Learning to cope with adversity and suffering builds strength. What is important are not the circumstances that befall us, but how we respond to those circumstances. The key question is not "Is the path easy?", but, "Is the path worthwhile?" Periodically stop and access your significant experiences, good and bad, and ask:

- "What did I learn from that?"
- "How can I use what I've learned to keep making progress?"

We're here to add something, to construct, to preserve. To leave something good for those little ones who are going to come into our world. Let that motivation be so firmly established in your heart and mind that you can say, "I will stand for this. I will live for this."
  Bear Heart – Muskogee Creek

In Viktor Frankl's book, *Man's Search for Meaning*, about the plight of Jews in the Nazi death camps of World War II, Frankl relates that he survived, but lost his wife and parents to the atrocities. From that experience, Frankl, a psychotherapist, developed a thesis that contends that others can control everything about a person but that person's attitude.

Frankl credited his survival, and that of others who survived, to adhering to the principles of:

- choosing an undefeated attitude.
- committing to values and goals.
- fulfilling one's responsibilities.
- serving others.
- demonstrating courage.
- seeking peace.
- pursuing happiness in the face of adversity.

Later he stressed these principles in his psychotherapy practice and espoused them in his writings.

Don't go after happiness; rather commit yourself to something bigger than yourself, and let happiness come chasing after you.

- Viktor Frankl

Define your purpose and write it down.

CHAPTER 13 - DEVELOP LIFE GOALS and OBJECTIVES

To determine how to live, we must first decide what we are living for. Defining clear personal goals and objectives keeps you focused on who you want to be and what you want to accomplish. Goal setting is the first step in turning the intangible into the tangible. Your most important goals and objectives are those which define the kind of person you want to <u>be</u>. Focus your goals on what you want to become.

> *People with goals succeed because they know where they're going.* - Earl Nightingale

A. Goals - are statements (decisions) about what you want from life. Your goals should include statements about the kind of person you want to be (I want to be a good student), what you want to accomplish (I want to write a book about making life-shaping decisions), and what you want to experience (I want to visit all the US National Parks). Goals are longer term and more general than objectives. Goals should establish the direction and parameters for your life. <u>Goals should incorporate your values.</u> When determining goals, it is useful to test them against your statements of values, and vice versa, to assure that they are consistent. Inconsistencies may warrant modifications to one or the other. That's ok. Inconsistencies aren't. Goals should reflect what you love, what is really important to you.

B. Objectives - define <u>results</u> to be accomplished in specific, measurable terms, with specified due dates. Always ask: what are the end results that I want? The attainment of objectives provides the building blocks for the accomplishment of goals. Objectives are end results to be achieved within a certain period of time. To be effective determinants of personal accomplishments, goals and objectives must be integrated, i.e., they must be consistent and mutually supportive. The attainment of objectives must lead to the accomplishment of goals, which, in turn, fulfill your personal purpose.

The following examples of goals and objectives illustrate the distinction between them:

Goal: I want to be a good father.

Related Objective: Starting this weekend, I will plan and engage in an activity with Joey, every weekend, for an uninterrupted duration of at least two hours.

Related Objective: I will read to Joey every evening.

Goal: I want to help relieve life's burdens for those less fortunate.

Related Objective: By the end of this month I will select a social services agency to which I will commit at least six hours of effort every month.

Goals and objectives are not just for businesses. It is useful to think about goals and objectives for each area of your life:

1. Family
2. Physical & Health
3. Career
4. Spiritual
5. Moral & Ethical
6. Financial
7. Mental & Educational

C. Write Them Down

It is imperative to write down the goals and objectives. Writing forces you to think about and clarify your targets. It also increases the probability of reaching your goals. Various research studies have found that those who write their goals and objectives are from three to nine times as likely to achieve them as those who don't. Whether the most accurate multiplier is three or nine is not important. The fact is that writing them down significantly increases the probability of achieving them.

> *You control your future, your destiny. What you think about, comes about. By recording your dreams and goals on paper, you set in motion the process of becoming the person you most want to be. Put your future in good hands – your own.*
> - Mark Victor Hansen

D. Some Other Guidelines for Developing Goals and Objectives:

1. **Personalize** - Assure that your goals are things you really want, not just statements designed to impress someone. Goals are personal. Make them yours.

2. **Be Specific** - Make your goal and objective statements definitive. Identify exactly what you want, in as much detail as possible.

3. **Be Realistic** – Goals and objectives should be attainable. They should require stretch but be possible. The right amount of stretch is a tough call. You should be looking for the right balance of challenge and reason. Many err by aiming too low. We tend to underestimate our potentials. However, consistently missing unrealistically high targets can frustrate and discourage. Construct some goals you are reasonably certain of attaining. Success builds confidence and confidence generates more success.

4. **Measure** - Find a way to make goals and objectives measurable. Not all will be quantifiable. Use numbers if you can, but if numbers don't fit, find another yardstick. It's hard to put a number on attaining a specific diploma, degree, certificate or license, but when you hold the document with your name on it in your hand; you know you've accomplished something. Measurements are important for indicating when you've hit your target, and equally important, for indicating progress. Use measurement to determine if you are really spending time on the things you have identified as important.

5. **Use Benchmarks** - For long term goals, establish benchmarks, (shorter term targets), to measure progress.

6. **Be Positive** - Write goal and objective statements in the positive rather than the negative. Use positive words like "achieve", "become" and "obtain" instead of "avoid" "reduce" or "less". Instead of declaring that you want to reduce the time you spend watching TV, state that you intend to read at least 18 thought provoking books per year. Instead of saying "I want to lose 13 pounds", say "I want to achieve a weight of 175 pounds and be able to run a mile in eight minutes by May 31."

7. **Be Consistent** - Assure that your goals are not conflicting or mutually exclusive. Test them against each other. If your goal is to be a social worker, it is not likely that you can realistically expect to live in an 18 room mansion with an ocean view, (unless you have another source of wealth).

8. **Set Dates** - Your targets should be time specific. Goals are typically long term and include what you want to be, so target dates can be more nebulous. Objectives should each have a clear target date for attainment.

9. **Focus** – Attainment is significantly dependent upon focused attention and effort. Problems with achievement can often be traced to lack of focus. Few of us can effectively pursue 15 objectives simultaneously. Prioritize and then stagger target dates to assure that attainment is realistic. Then really concentrate on a few high priorities.

10. **Share Selectively** – Goals and objectives are personal. Wide distribution invites expressions of skepticism and unreliable advice. Share them only with one to two people whose advice you trust, and ask those people to periodically review progress with you and hold you accountable.

11. **Review** – Keep goal and objective statements visible and review them periodically, (at least once or twice a month). For maximum effectiveness, internalize them to the extent that they are a part of your consciousness, for automatic reference when making serious decisions.

The most important benefit of setting and writing down goals doesn't come from the attainment of the goals, but from the self – awareness, discipline, and priorities established by going through the process. Taking goal and objective setting seriously can make a positive difference in your life, and testing decisions against goals and objectives can help you make significantly better decisions.

You should aim high when selecting goals, but consider not only the results you want but also the price you are willing to pay to achieve those results. You must realistically assess the effort, sacrifices, and the tradeoffs necessary to realize a particular dream. High personal costs should not automatically dissuade you from pursuing a goal. You should just be sure you understand the price and are willing to pay it.

> *When we are motivated by goals that have deep meaning, by dreams that need completion, by pure love that needs expressing, then we truly live.*
> - Greg Anderson

Goals and objectives clarify purpose and fuel your capacity to accomplish. Be sure your goals and objectives include not only the ends you wish to achieve, but also include statements about the **process**, those things you must do to achieve the goal. Goals alone are not enough. Each team in an athletic contest has "winning" as a goal. The one who prevails will be the one who has the determination to do the work, and exercises the discipline, to do what it takes to win.

Recognize that achievement is the result of continuous self-improvement, not a sudden, remarkable transformation. Outcomes are a function of who you are, the processes you employ, and your effort.

Developing goals and objectives is important to the accomplishment of any endeavor, but merely developing them is not the end. Having established goals and objectives, it is imperative to ask: What do I have to know and learn to achieve them? How do I learn what I need to know? What do I have to <u>do</u> to achieve them? Without the required knowledge and a plan of action, goals become wishes with little chance of realization.

When making important decisions, always consider whether a course of action enhances or impedes your ability to achieve your goals and objectives.

Please read and think about the story in Case Study 13, "Gabby on Values, Character and Goals," at the end of this chapter.

CASE STUDY 13 - "GABBY", ON VALUES, CHARACTER AND GOALS

As I was revising the manuscript for this book in August of 2024, the Olympics, in Paris France, had just concluded. One of the major highlights for Americans was the success story of Gabrielle, "Gabby" Thomas. Gabby won three gold medals in track competition, one solo, in the 200 meter event, and two as a member of winning relay teams.

Gabby attributes her success as an athlete, and as a person, to the values and character instilled in her by her mother.

Her mother, Jennifer Randall, grew up in poverty in Mobile, Alabama. Starting as a waitress, she earned bachelor's and master's degrees from Duke University, and a PhD from Emory University. She became a teacher, first at the high school level, then as an associate professor at the University of Massachusetts. She is currently an endowed chair professor at the University of Michigan and the founder and chairperson of a non-profit foundation supporting education for minority students.

Gabby indicates that her "Mum" has been the best role model a person could have, and has always been supportive, encouraging, and inspirational. "As a single mom, she raised me to value hard work, education, and giving back to the community. Watching how hard she worked showed me that you can achieve your dreams if you are willing to work. As my athletic accomplishments grew, she kept reminding me of the importance of education. She showed me that education was a way of leveling the playing field. I'm trying to follow in her footsteps. I have confidence that if I follow the values she taught, and work hard, I can achieve what I want to achieve."

"We were low income and African American. But my Mum was trying to set us up to be successful, which meant we were in primarily white spaces, going to good schools. That put an underdog mentality in me, where I felt like I needed to prove that I belonged in every space that I was in."

When the family moved to Massachusetts, Jennifer enrolled Gabby in a "white space" prep school. She excelled academically and began to demonstrate athletic abilities. She chose Harvard University to further her education, because of its reputation for academic excellence and because of the challenge it represented. She was accepted and graduated with a degree in neurobiology. "Having to prove myself academically at Harvard made me fight more in other social settings, and especially on the track." While at Harvard, she began to excel as a sprinter. She later earned a master's degree in public health from the University of Texas, in Austin.

Gabby's athletic accomplishments are outstanding. While at Harvard, she won 22 conference titles, in six different events, in only three years. (she gave up her fourth year of eligibility, but completed her degree). She owns Ivy League and Harvard records in the 100 meters, 200 meters, and indoor 60 meters. She won a bronze medal in the 200 meters and a silver as part of a relay team, at the 2020 Olympics in Japan. In 2023, she won the U S National Championship in the 200 meters and was second in that event at the World Athletics Championship. Her three golds in the 2024 Olympics cap her athletic achievements to date.

Gabby attributes her speed to her father's genes. He is from Jamaica and was a defensive back on the Duke University football team.

Gabby believes in the power of stepping outside her comfort zone and setting goals. She accomplished her goal of being accepted into, and graduating from, a challenging university. She set and achieved the goal of qualifying for the U S Olympic Team in 2020. She then set her sights on gold in the 2024 Games. Been there, done that. She is pondering the 2028 Olympics.

She has goals beyond athletics. She hopes one day to be chief executive of a hospital and to start her own non-profit foundation, for the improvement of public health. She understands the dynamics of her mother's childhood experience as one of numerous siblings in a household with insufficient resources and restricted access to adequate doctors and healthcare. She wants to make a difference.

Gabby is an advocate of activity, giving back, and balance. She practices what she preaches. Her mother says she is never happy unless she has multiple balls in the air. She did a remarkable job of balancing education and athletics at Harvard and the University of Texas. She balances her six to eight hours of training per day with volunteering at a health care clinic for people who don't have health insurance. She says the change of pace, doing something entirely different, refreshes her and makes her more effective at both.

During one summer break from Harvard, she had an experience that she says changed her life. She moved to Dakar, Senegal, to study that nation's culture and religion. She found that, although the people had less money and fewer possessions than Americans, they seemed far happier. They appeared more connected to each other, more pleasant, more willing to help. She gained a new perspective about what things matter most. Her mother said it was a transformative experience. "She came back brand new."

Gabby loves life. She says she loves sports and competing as an Olympian, because it builds character and permits her to live the values her mother taught and demonstrated. She loves learning, and she loves giving. She insists that these values have brought her success in her life way beyond athletics.

What are the core values that Gabby admires and practices?

_____

_____

_____

What character traits does she demonstrate?

_____

_____

_____

What obstacles have Gabby had to overcome?

_____

_____

How has setting goals helped her overcome obstacles?

_____

_____

_____

CHAPTER 14 – DEVELOP A PERSONAL MISSION STATEMENT

Among the most useful things you can do to take control of your life, become the person you want to be, and have the potential to be, is to prepare a personal mission statement. The mission statement is a compilation of your values, principles, goals, objectives, and the character traits by which you plan to live. It is your personal "constitution," the expression of who you are, the criteria against which you will measure your life activities.

The process is as important as the product. It encourages you to think through your priorities and to align your behavior with your beliefs. It is not something to do casually, or whip out in a few minutes. It takes careful reflection, analysis, conscious decision-making, and usually several revisions, to refine it to the point where it is useful, and you are comfortable with it. It is worth the effort. There are many benefits.

A. Benefits to Writing a Personal Mission Statement.

1. It helps you focus on who you want to be (your character) and what you want to do (accomplish and contribute).
2. It helps you clarify what is really important to you
3. It helps you make decisions.
4. It helps you identify reasons for doing what you're doing.
5. It helps you decide what you like and what you're good at.
6. It helps you establish standards, what you will do, and what you won't do.
7. It helps you decide whether or not to go along with the herd.
8. It helps you cope with change.

9. It helps you develop a script and a roadmap for your life.
10. It helps you identify opportunities for learning and contribution.

B. The Process

1. Complete the "Preparation for Writing a Personal Mission Statement" exercise in Appendix Q.
2. Review your values, principles, and the character traits you wish to develop, and incorporate them into the statement. Start by simply listing, and then refine your list of values, principles, and character traits into a definition of who you want to be.
3. Review your list of wonts.
4. Start with a very rough draft. Don't try to make it perfect.
5. Review and re-write.
6. Make it you.
7. Ignore labels others try to place on you.
8. Don't try to make it fit someone else's expectations. It is your personal "constitution."
9. Don't ask yourself if it's perfect, but rather, "Does it move me in the right direction?"
10. Ask yourself if it inspires you to be a better you.

For reference, there is a list of representative elements from mission statements provided in Appendix R. Note that this list does not represent someone's actual mission statement, nor is it intended for you to copy. It represents a composite of actual components, and paraphrases of actual components, I have seen in personal mission statements. It is provided to stimulate your thinking.

PART VII - CHOOSE TO MAKE YOUR LIFE MEANINGFUL

The heading for this section raises the question of; "What is at the heart of the word "meaning?" As it applies to your life, it involves understanding three concepts: Coherence – things happen for a reason; Purpose – I am alive in order to do something; Significance – my life matters.

Finding meaning includes seeking wisdom and doing the right thing. Wisdom is about more than thinking. A life of meaning involves choosing to live wisely, aligning actions with valid values and principles, learning and evolving as a person, and contributing something useful to the world.

CHAPTER 15 – CHOOSE TO BE A BETTER YOU

Life is an endless quest, a search for wisdom and for experiences that enlighten. Finding meaning and purpose takes effort, introspection, and wise choices about principles and values. It means being open to direction from a Higher Intelligence, searching inside for the real you. It involves deciding what kind of person you choose to be and what kind of life you want to live.

> *The value of life lies not in the length of days, but in the use we make of them; a man may live long yet live very little.*
> *- Michel de Montaigne*

In the end, meaning is very personal. We each have a responsibility to determine a purpose for our lives that has significance for us. A part of that task is to develop yourself into the most wise, moral, strong, and loving person you can be, and to live in peace with a clear conscience. At the same time, you must understand that a "good" life is a process, not a state of being. You cannot be perfect.

We are visitors on this planet. We are here for ninety, a hundred years at the very most. During that time we must try to do something good, something useful with our lives. Try to be at peace with yourself and help others share that peace. If you contribute to other people's happiness, you will find the true goal, the meaning of life.
    - The Dalai Lama

The key to becoming who you want to be is to never stop making small improvements. You do not need to achieve an overnight transformation. The small changes you make don't just add up, they compound. It is remarkable what you can accomplish if you just keep improving.

CHAPTER 16 – LET YOUR LIFE SPEAK

The real you is revealed, not by what you believe, or what you profess, but by what you do. Let the way you live your life demonstrate who you are. Doing good enables you to be good and to feel good.

A. Where there is hatred, demonstrate love.

B. Where there is injury, learn to forgive.

C. Where there is sadness, promote joy.

D. Where there is despair, show hope.

E. Where there is strife, become an instrument of peace.

F. Strive to understand the point of view of others.

G. Commit to truth.

H. Practice integrity.

I. Live ethically and morally.

J. Serve others.

K. Search for understanding and wisdom.

L. Keep the important things first.

M. Treat people with kindness and compassion.

N. Support justice and fairness for all.

CHAPTER 17 – CHOOSE TO REALLY LIVE

Life is a gift. Use it well.

Henry David Thoreau wrote that he wanted: "to front only the essential facts of life, and see if I could learn what it had to teach, and not, when I came to die, to discover that I had not lived."

He chose to live. So should you. The world is a wonderful and mysterious place. It offers more possibilities than we can ever conceive. Try some of them.

> *Difficult times have helped me understand better than before how infinitely rich and beautiful life is in every way, and that so many things that one goes worrying about are of no importance whatsoever.*
> *- Isak Dinesen*

Make a decision to make better decisions. Making better decisions will improve the quality of your life. One of the most important, fundamental, decisions that you can make is to decide to live your life, not just take up time and space, but <u>really live</u>.

> Imagine you only have 10 hours to live. What would you do?
>
> Imagine you only have 10 days to live. What would you do?
>
> Imagine you only have 10 months to live. What would you do?

Contemplate your answers to these questions. What would you do differently if you knew the exact amount of life you had left? How would you redesign/refocus your life? Assuming that you would do something differently, why should not knowing the duration of your life keep you from starting that redesign _now_, from changing your focus _now_?

> *None of us know how much time we have to live, but we know it is finite. However long or short it is, we should live it to maximize: the joy of family and friends, service to others, and making the most of our potential. It's only when we truly know and understand that we have a limited time on earth – and that we have no way of knowing when our time is up – that we will begin to live each day to the fullest, as if it was the only one we had.*
> - Elizabeth Kübler-Ross

Develop a bias for action. Live life, don't just let it happen. DO SOMETHING to:

1. Ease the burdens of others.
2. Help others grow and realize their potential.
3. Demonstrate kindness.
4. Mold your character to align with valid values and principles.
5. Learn, grow and realize your personal potential.
6. Make something beautiful.
7. Teach someone something useful.
8. Promote social fairness and justice.
9. Improve relationships between people.
10. Preserve the wonder and beauty of nature.

It is in _doing_ these things that we find meaning.

One of my favorite observations about life was written by George Bernard Shaw:

> *Life is no brief candle to me. It is a sort of splendid torch which I have got a hold of for the moment, and I want to make it burn as brightly as possible before handing it on to future generations. I want to be thoroughly used up when I die, for the harder I work, the more I live. I rejoice in life for its own sake. This is the true joy of life: being used for a purpose recognized by yourself as a worthy one, being thoroughly worn out before being thrown on the scrap heap, being a force of nature instead of a selfish little clod of ailments and grievances complaining that the world will not devote itself to making you happy.*

Every day, do something to make you a better you. Every day, learn something new. Every day, demonstrate compassion for someone. Every day, take time to relax and enjoy life. Regularly ask yourself, Am I becoming the person I want to be?

LIFE LESSONS

If it's not yours, don't take it.
If it's not true, don't say it.
if it's not right, don't do it.
If it's not healthful, don't consume it.

Choose to live, really live.
Live well, love much, laugh often.

Demonstrate compassion. Find ways to serve.

Count your blessings and be grateful.

Recognize and appreciate the beauty that surrounds you;
in nature, in people, in life.

Never stop learning.

Choose to do something worthwhile.
Whatever you choose to do, aim high, be brave, be strong,
believe that you can succeed.

Be honest with yourself and others.
Ensure that what you know, say, and do, are consistent

Be conscientious. Do what you commit to do.

Be persistent. Finish what you start.

Seek Truth

Seek Wisdom

LIFE IS PRECIOUS! CHOOSE TO REALLY LIVE IT.
THIS IS NOT A REHEARSAL.

APPENDIX A

CLARIFYING VALUES

The following is a list of personal values cited by persons asked about such things. Add to the list any others that you consider important to you. There are no right or wrong answers.

Circle the 15 – 24 that you consider most important

Accountability	Security/ Safety	Status
Perseverance/ Tenacity	Self Confidence	Family
Compassion	Community	Peace
Achievement	Goodness	Fun
Wealth	Gratitude	Financial Security
Compassion	Ambition	Integrity/Honesty
Balance/ Harmony	Work Ethic	Leisure
Calmness	Assertiveness	Physical Safety
Commitment	Belonging	Independence
Freedom	Kindness	Happiness
Dependability	Cooperation	Contentment
Fairness/Justice	Spirituality	Physical Fitness
Friendship	Creativity	Personal Growth
Faith	Health	Freedom
Generosity	Serving Others	Pleasure
Respect	Stability	Honor
Competitiveness	Challenge	Independence

Consistency	Love	Reliability/Dependability
Excitement	Stability	Being Organized
Fame	Teamwork	Learning/Education
Contribution	Intelligence	Beauty
Courtesy	Respect for Nature	Artistic Expression
Creativity	Enjoyment	Morality
Decisiveness	Self-Control	Conservation
Quality/Excellence	Responsibility	Loyalty
Empathy	Success	Truthfulness
Conscientiousness	Courage	Ethics
Authenticity	Popularity	Trust
Human Worth/Dignity/Inclusiveness		Wisdom

Other _____

Other _____

Other _____

APPENDIX B

PRIORITIZING VALUES

Divide your personal values list from Appendix A into three categories

1. CRITICAL   _____
                     _____
                     _____
                     _____
                     _____
                     _____
                     _____
                     _____

2. VERY IMPORTANT   _____
                     _____
                     _____
                     _____
                     _____
                     _____
                     _____
                     _____

3. IMPORTANT   _____
                     _____
                     _____
                     _____
                     _____
                     _____

APPENDIX C

EXAMPLES of VALUES AND RELATED PRINCIPLES

VALUE	RELATED PRINCIPLES
Integrity/ Honesty	I will not lie, cheat, or steal
Empathy	I will seek to understand the feelings and needs of others by mentaly and emotionally "putting myself in their shoes"
Compassion	I will find ways to help those with emotional and physical needs.
Fairness/Justice	I will treat all persons and situations with fairness and suport causes of genuine fairness and justice.
Human Worth/Inclusiveness	I will treat all persons with dignity and respect, regardless of race, religion or national origin.
Health	I will not take dangrous drugs, smoke, or drink alcohol, or if I drink alcohol, I will limit my consumption to one drink per day. I will exercise regularly.

Responsibility	I will always accept responsibility for my decisions and my actions.
Truth	I will seek, and always tell, the truth.
Courage	I will strive to do what is right regardles of danger, criticism, personal hardship, or popular opinion.
Wisdom	I will strive to attain the knowledge, good judgement, and ethics necessary to make wise decisions.
Perserverance/Tenacity	I will strive to develop the personal strength to overcome adversity and achieve objectives in the face of opposition and hardship.
Conscientiousness	I will strive to be dependable, do what I say I will do, be there when others need me, and do quality work.
Respect	I will always treat others as I want to be treated.

Service	I will consciously invest time in efforts to benefit others.
Self Control	I will choose thoughtful, rational responses to external forces. I will avoid impulsive, self-destructive reactions to temptations, threats, addictions, and provocations.
Family	I will love, honor and support my family.
Friendship	I will choose my friends carefully and strive to be supportive and a positive influence for the friends I choose.
Self Determinination/ Personal Choices	I will make my own choices. I will not permit peers to convince me to do things that I think are wrong.
Morality/Ethics	I will strive to do what is "right", treat people fairly, and do no harm.

Kindness	I will strive to be attentive, considerate, empathetic, friendly, and helpful.
Work	I will view work as an opportunity to learn, grow and demonstrate my capability.
Gratitude	I will strive to appreciate what I have and express thanks for all I receive.
Nature	I will make environmental sustainability and preservation a conscious part of my decision making.
Learning	I will strive to maintain curiosity and a learning mindset, recognizing that every experience has something to teach me.
Loyalty	I will strive to demonstrate allegence to family, friends, country, and just causes.

APPENDIX D
MY VALUES AND RELATED PRINCIPLES

VALUE		RELATED PRINCIPLES
Integrity/ Honesty		I will not lie, cheat, or steal

VALUE		RELATED PRINCIPLES

APPENDIX E

A NOTE ABOUT USING CASE STUDIES

To help you appreciate the benefits of thinking about values, principles, and character, the text suggests at intervals that you reflect on "case studies" that highlight these issues. Some of the cases are inspirational, to demonstrate that one can overcome adversities. Some are descriptions of difficult situations that encourage you to think of what you would do if confronted with the decision maker's dilemma.

Case studies are descriptions of actual situations in which people are confronted with choices. The person involved must determine the relevant facts, develop alternatives, and make decisions. The objective in asking you to consider these stories is to provide you with an opportunity to think, to make decisions when the stakes are neutral, so you will learn to make better decisions when the stakes are personal and high. Reflecting on cases provides an opportunity to apply what you have selected as your values, your principles, and desired character traits, to real life situations.

To attain the maximum benefit from using case studies, you need to put yourself in the shoes of the decision maker, determine the relevant facts, develop practical alternatives and decide what you would do in the situation. Think about the questions posed at the end of each case, and especially think about what you would do if it was you in the situation. It is useful to work with a pencil and paper to help organize your thoughts, and to note the values, principles and character traits you are applying.

APPENDIX F

SELECTING CHARACTER ATTRIBUTES/TRAITS

THE CHARACTER TRAITS I WANT TO BUILD INTO MY CHARACTER.

1. _____
2. _____
3. _____
4. _____
5. _____
6. _____
7. _____
8. _____
9. _____
10. _____
11. _____
12. _____
13. _____
14. _____
15. _____

APPENDIX G

OPPORTUNITIES TO SERVE

1. Visit someone in a nursing home
2. Volunteer at your local animal shelter
3. Organize a Park cleanup with friends.
4. Help with yard work for elderly or unwell neighbors
5. Volunteer at a local soup kitchen
6. Become a mentor to a young person
7. Volunteer at an after school program
8. Donate your hair to charities like Wigs for Kids or Children With Hair Loss
9. Donate blood at the Red Cross
10. Collect and donate gently used coats and sweatshirts to a local charity
11. Teach English as a second language as a literacy volunteer
12. Tutor students
13. Volunteer to help build homes with Habitat for Humanity.
14. Register to become an organ donor
15. Volunteer at an equine therapy center
16. Coach a local youth team
17. Volunteer at Meals on Wheels
18. Volunteer at a hospital
19. Recycle
20. Volunteer at a wilderness center
21. Volunteer to read to kids at the local library, nursery, or preschool
22. Collect food to donate to food pantries
23. Volunteer at a local non-profit agency. Check with the United Way for suggestions and contacts

24. Organize a fund raising event for a local charity
25. Volunteer with an adaptive sports program
26. _____
27. _____
28. _____
29. _____
30. _____

The activity to which I commit to become involved within the next two weeks:

_____

Date: _____

APPENDIX H

NAMES OF OTHERS WHO WOULD BE AFFECTED BY MY ADDICTION

Drug use is not just about you. Others would inevitably be affected. In the spaces below list the names of those who could be affected, if you became addicted or became a "user".

1. _____
2. _____
3. _____
4. _____
5. _____
6. _____
7. _____
8. _____
9. _____
10. _____
11. _____
12. _____

APPENDIX I

A PERSONAL PLEDGE TO MYSELF

I understand that illegal drugs, marijuana, nicotine and alcohol are all drugs, are mind and body altering substances, and potential killers.

I understand that my use of these substances can have harmful effects on me, my family, my friends and total strangers.

I CHOOSE to maintain personal control over my mind and body.

I THEREFORE PLEDGE THAT:

____ I will never use illegal drugs.

____ I will never use marijuana.

____ I will never use products containing nicotine.

____ I will never drink alcoholic beverages.

OR

____ If I drink alcoholic beverages, I will limit my consumption to one drink per day.

X _____ (Signature)

Date _____

APPENDIX J

FRAMING WORKSHEET

Why is a Decision Required? What are the Root Causes of the Issue?

What is the Real Issue?

How Important is the Issue?   Comments

☐ 1 Paramount
☐ 2 Significant
☐ 3 Material
☐ 4 Mundane

What Are the Real Needs?

What Are My Objectives?
Primary:

Secondary:

What Are the Real Constraints?

What Are My Relevant Personal Preferences?

By When Should the Decision Be Made?
    Required Date _____
    Target Date _____

Comments

APPENDIX K

DECISION CONSEQUENCES WORKSHEET				
Description of the Issue				
Alternative #	1	2	3	4
Alternative Description				
Likely Positive Outcomes				
Probability				
Likely Negative Outcomes				
Probability				
Values Reinforced				
Goals/Objectives Supported				

For the likely outcomes assign a Probability from 1% to 100%

APPENDIX L

IMPACT ON OTHERS WORKSHEET				
Description of the Issue				
Alternative #	1	2	3	4
Alternative Description				
Person/Group Impacted				
Likely Positive Impacts				
Likely Negative Impacts				

APPENDIX M

A CHECKLIST FOR REVIEWING YOUR PROCESS FOR MAKING MAJOR DECISIONS

Before "pulling the trigger" on a major decision, think it through:

1. Is the issue adequately defined? Have I identified the real need?
2. Are my objectives clearly defined and will attaining the objectives satisfy the real need?
3. Is my assessment of the importance of the decision accurate?
4. Have I identified the constraints accurately?
5. Have I accurately described my personal feelings and preferences? Can I objectively assess their impact on the decision?
6. Do I have the information required to make an effective decision?
7. Have I objectively eliminated unacceptable alternatives?
8. Have I creatively and realistically identified the feasible alternatives?
9. Have I adequately anticipated the consequences of each alternative?
10. Have I adequately considered the impact of each alternative on other people?
11. Have I adequately evaluated the consistency of each alternative with my values?

12. Have I adequately evaluated the consistency of each alternative with my goals and objectives?

13. If probabilities are involved in my analysis, have I included all possible options and realistically estimated probabilities?

Some Tips for Thinking Through Alternative Solutions

- Someone, somewhere has dealt with this issue or solved this problem before (or one very similar). You don't always have to "reinvent the wheel." Sometimes "best practices" are best practices for a reason, they work. Search for those solutions and determine if one or more can be adapted to your situation. (search the internet, reference books, query experts, etc.).

- Have you faced a similar situation before? Analyze what worked and/or what didn't?

- Break down the issue or problem into segments, deal with the segments individually, and combine viable solutions.

- If there is one particularly difficult element to the issue, separate it out. Apply the most rigorous analysis to that element. Having solved it, the rest become easier. If you can't solve it, don't waste time on the other elements.

- Combine two or more alternatives to build a "better" one.

- Consider "inverting" the elements of a possible solution. Change the sequence of steps to see if that improves the solution.

- Examine the possibility of using a potentially negative consequence of an option to create a positive effect that cancels out the negative.

- Identify ways to test the option before committing.

- If cost is a constraint, evaluate ways to reduce the costs through: substitution, removing non-essentials, changing time schedules, changing sources, modifying specifications, etc.

Check your conclusions against all available evidence.

APPENDIX N					
IMPLEMENTATION PLAN WORKSHEET				
ACTION	By Whom	By When	Tools/Resources Required	Who To Involve

APPENDIX O   DECISION REVIEW LOG

POST MORTEMS - EVALUATING PAST DECISIONS

Date _____

Issue as Defined: _____

Targeted Outcome: _____

Actual Outcome: _____

Reasons for Differences _____

What did I learn about? What would I do differently about:

Framing the Issue? _____

Gathering information? _____

Identifying Alternatives? _____

Considering Consequenses? _____

Impact on Others? _____

Thinking it Through? _____

If I were making the decision today, I would: _____

APPENDIX P

SUGGESTED READING LIST
Books that entertain and enlighten, with themes that illustrate Values, Principles and Character

The Adventures of Huckleberry Finn
    Mark Twain

The Call of the Wild
    Jack London

David Copperfield
    Charles Dickens

Emily of New Moon
    L. M. Montgomery

A Girl of the Limberlost
    Gene Stratton Porter

The Grapes of Wrath
    John Steinbeck

Great Expectations
    Charles Dickens

Jayne Eyre
    Charlotte Bronte

The Last of the Mohicans
    James Fenimore Cooper

Moby Dick
    Herman Melville

Robinson Crusoe
    Daniel Defoe

Roll of Thunder, Hear My Cry
    Mildred D. Taylor

The Scarlet Pimpernel
    Baroness Emmuska Orczy

Dear Martin
    Nic Stone

Silas Marner
    George Eliot

Typhoon and Other Tales
    Joseph Conrad

Maniac Magee
    Jerry Spinelli

Bridge to Terabithia
    Katherine Paterson

The Chosen
    Chaim Potok

Dicey's Song
    Cynthia Voigt

My Antonia
  Willa Cather

One Corpse Too Many
  Ellis Peters

How to Change Everything
  Naomi Klein, Rebecca Stefoff

The Prisoner of Zenda
  Anthony Hope

Clara Barton: Founder of the American Red Cross
  Susan Sloate

Louis Braille: The Boy Who Invented Books for the Blind
  Margaret Davidson

Frederick Douglas: Voice of Freedom
  Eric Weiner

Amelia Earhart: Pioneer of the Sky
  John Parlin

Martin Luther King, Jr. Dreams for a Nation
  Louise Quayle

Magellan: First Around the World
  Ronald Syme

Hatchet
  Gary Paulsen

The Planet of Junior Brown
  Virginia Hamilton

Jim Abbott: All-American Pitcher
  Howard Reiser

The Great Little Madison
  Jean Fritz

The 7 Habits of Highly Effective Teens
  Sean Covey

George Washington: The Man Who Would Not Be King
  Stephen Krensky

Martin Luther
  May McNeer and Lynd Ward

The Diary of a Young Girl
  Anne Frank

Harriet and the Runaway Book: The Story of Harriet Beecher Stowe
  Johanna Johnston

Jim Thorpe: Olympic Champion
  Guernsey Van Riper, Jr.

A Deaf Child Listened: Thomas Gallaudet, Pioneer in American Education
    Anne Neimark

A Tree Grows in Brooklyn
    Betty Smith

Go Tell It On the Mountain
    James Baldwin

Angela's Ashes
    Frank McCort

The Absolute True Diary of a Part Time Indian
    Sherman Alexie

Jesse Owens: Champion Athlete
    Rick Rennert

Little Women
    Louisa May Alcott

A Separate Peace
    John Knowles

The Hunger Games
    Suzanne Collins

The House on Mango Street
    Sandra Cisneros

APPENDIX Q

THINKING ABOUT THE PERSON YOU WANT TO BE
Preparation For Writing Your Personal Mission Statement

List seven things you genuinely enjoy doing.

1 _____
2 _____
3 _____
4 _____
5 _____
6 _____
7 _____

List Four Times in Your Life When You Really Felt Motivated To Do Something. What Motivated You?

1 _____
2 _____
3 _____
4 _____

List The Names of Three Persons (dead or alive), that you Really Respect. What are the Qualities That You Admire?

	Name	Qualities
1	_____	_____
		_____
2	_____	_____
		_____
3	_____	_____
		_____

If You Could Take a Free Two Day Course About Any Subject You Chose, About What Would You Like To Learn?

1 _____

2 _____

3 _____

What Are Your Greatest Personal Strengths?

1 _____

2 _____

3 _____

4 _____

If in Thirty Years Your Friends and Work Associates Were Being Interviewed For a Story About You, What Would You Want Them to Say?

1 _____

2 _____

3 _____

4 _____

What Characteristics Do You Consider Most Important When Selecting Friends?

1 _____

2 _____

3 _____

4 _____

APPENDIX R - MISSION STATEMENT EXAMPLES

WHAT I CHOOSE TO BE:

Honest – I will not lie, cheat or steal.

Fair – I will treat others fairly and with justice, as I wish to be treated.

Compassionate – I will seek ways to help and support people with problems.

Responsible – I will accept responsibility for my words and actions.

Kind – I will be attentive, generous, considerate and supportive.

Conscientious – I will strive to do well what I choose to do.

Inclusive – I will treat all people with dignity and respect, regardless of race, or religion.

Dependable – I will do what I commit to do.

Physically Fit – I will respect and take good care of my body.

Grateful – I will demonstrate appreciation for my many blessings.

Friendly – I will strive to be there for those I choose as friends.

Loyal – I will strive to support family, friends, and country.

WHAT I PLAN TO DO:

Graduate from college.

Select a vocation that is worthwhile and provides a sense of accomplishment and satisfaction.

Become actively involved in a project and/or one or more organizations that help people.

Become actively involved in a hobby that requires physical activity, e.g., tennis or softball.

Visit a least five foreign countries to learn about other cultures.

Develop at least one new proficiency per year.

Become a competent nature photographer.

Engage in at least one major personal education project per year.

Develop a personal relationship with at least one person of another race.

Develop a personal relationship with at least one person of another religion.

Support family.

Learn to manage my finances effectively.

Proactively pursue my goals and objectives.

Support efforts to sustain nature and wilderness.

Love life, family, learning, and the earth.

I will not use drugs, alcohol, or nicotine.

Learn to be a competent piano player.

(Note that the above does not represent any one mission statement. It is a composite of actual components, and paraphrases of actual components, from mission statements I have seen. Its purpose is to stimulate your thinking.)

BIBLIOGRAPHY

Bauer, Gary. *Our Journey Home, What Parents Are Doing To Preserve Family Values.* Dallas, TX. World Publishing, 1992.

Bennet, William J. *The Book of Virtues.* New York, NY. Simon & Schuster, 1993.

Brooks, Arthur C., and Oprah Winfrey. *Build the Life You Want.* New York, NY. Portfolio/Penguin, 2023.

Brooks, David. *The Road to Character.* New York, NY. Random House, 2015

Canfield, Jack. *The Success Principles.* New York, NY. Harper Collins, 2005.

Carter, Jimmy. *Our Endangered Values.* New York, NY. Simon & Schuster, 2005.

Clark, Kate Stevenson. *Handling Peer Pressure.* New York, NY. Chelsea House, 2009.

Clear, James. *Atomic Habits, Tiny Changes, Remarkable Results.* New York, NY. Avery, 2018.

Cloud, Dr. Henry & Dr. John Townsend. *Boundaries.* Grand Rapids, MI. Zondervan, 2017.

Covey, Sean. *The 7 Habits of Highly Effective Teens.* New York, NY. Fireside, 1988.

-----------------. *The 6 Most Important Decisions You'll Ever Make.* New York, NY. Fireside, 2006.

Covey, Stephen R. *The 7 Habits of Highly Effective People.* New York, NY. Simon & Schuster, 1989.

Dent, Harry S. *Teaching Jack & Jill Right Vs Wrong In The Homes & Schools.* Columbia, SC. Self-Published, 1996.

Desetta, AL. ed. *The Courage To Be Yourself.* Minneapolis, MN. Free Spirit Publishing, Inc., 2005

Dosick, Wayne. *Golden Rules: The Ten Ethical Values Parents Need To Teach Their Children.* New York, NY. Harper Paperbacks, 1998

Edwards, Josephine Cunnington. *Teaching Old-Fashioned Values to New-Fashioned Kids.* Hagerstown, MD. Review & Herald Publishing Association, 1992.

Eyre, Linda and Richard. *Teaching Your Children Values.* New York, NY. Fireside, 1993.

Felton, Edward L. Jr. *Living Our Values.* Cleveland, TN. Ethicos Press, 2011.

----------------------------. *Ethics and Values in Your Personal Life.* New York, NY. Harper Paperbacks, 1995.

Greer, Colin & Herbert Kohl, eds. *A Call to Character.* New York, NY. Harper Collins, 1995.

Gulla, Ashok. *Creating Values in Life.* Bloomington, IN. Author House, 2010.

Hanh, Thich Nhat. *The Miracle of Mindfulness, A Manual on Meditation.* Boston, MA. Beacon Press, 1976.

Hayden, Graham. *Teaching About Values.* London, GB. Cassell, 1997.

Holiday, Ryan. *The Obstacle Is The Way.* New York, NY. Penguin Group, 2014.

Kilpatrick, William, Gregory and Suzanne M. Wolfe. *Books That Build Character.* New York, NY. Touchstone, 1994.

Leman, Dr. Kevin. *Bringing Up Kids Without Tearing Them Down.* New York, NY. Delacorte Press, 1993.

Lewis, Hunter. *A Question of Values.* Crozet, VA. Axios Press, 1990.

McGraw, Phillip C. PhD. *Life Strategies. Doing What Works. Doing What Matters.* New York, NY. Hyperion, 1999.

Medoff, Lisa, Ph.D. *Stressed Out Students Guide To Handling Peer Pressure.* New York, NY. Kaplan Publishing, 2008.

Newman, Susan. *It Won't Happen To Me – True Stories of Teen Alcohol and Drug Abuse.* New York, NY. Perigee Books. 1987.

Newman, Susan. *You Can Say No To A Drink Or A Drug.* New York, NY. Perigee Books, 1986.

Rogers, Carl R. *On Becoming A Person.* Boston, MA. Houghton Mifflin, 1961.

Rosemond, John. *Teen-Proofing.* Kansas City, MO. Andrews McMeel Publishing, 2001.

Shirer, Larry. *Nelson T. Gant, From Slave to Prosperous Business Owner and Respected Citizen.* Seattle, WA. Kindle Direct Publishing, 2023.

Simon, Sidney B., Leland W. Howe, Howard Kirschenbaum. *Values Clarification.* New York, NY. Hart Publishing Company, Inc., 1972.

Townsend, Dr. John. *Boundaries With Teens.* Grand Rapids, MI. Zondervan, 2006.

Treager, Randy. *Building Character, One Virtue at a Time.* Sisters, OR. Deep River Books, 2014.

ABOUT THE AUTHOR

I'm a husband, father, grandfather, mentor, history buff, author and photographer.

I earned an MBA degree in Finance and Marketing from the Harvard Business School, and a BBA from Ohio University.

Serving as: Chairman of the Board of the United Way, Chairman of the Allocations Committee of the United Way, Chairman of the Board of a soup kitchen, Chairman of a church's Strategic Planning committee, a member of a Homelessness Task Force and as a Mentor to junior high and high school youth, all contributed to my education, as did helping my wife rear five offspring and joyfully observing the rearing of nine grandchildren.

Other books I've published include the following:

SOME THOUGHTS ABOUT LIFE – 2016

CHOICES – How to Make Better Decisions – 2018

POINTS TO PONDER – How to Live a Meaningful Life - 2020

WE ARE ALL RELATED – Life Lessons From Native American Wisdom – 2020

TEEN CHOICES – How to Make Better Decisions – 2021

ICONS OF OUR HERITAGE – 2022

DEALING WITH DIFFERENCES – 2023

NELSON T. GANT – From Slave to Prosperous Business Owner and Respected Citizen – 2023

NATIVE AMERICAN SPIRITUALITY and SACRED PLACES - 2024

All are available on Amazon and on the author's website at larrysbooksandphotos.com.

You may be wondering what this old turkey can possibly know about being a teenager. Believe it or not, about seventy years ago I was one. The world was different then. I realize that. I've learned some things since.

I learned by helping my wife rear five teenagers. I learned, later, by watching those five rear nine. I learned by serving as an advisor to a Junior Achievement group. I learned serving as a leader of a teenage Sunday School class. I learned by serving as a mentor to teens in our school system. I learned by teaching college courses part time. I learned by consulting with professionals who regularly deal with young people.

I learned by reading, a lot. In fact, I did extensive research about teen decision making and wrote an earlier book I call *Teen Choices*.

This book includes information from further research and includes the best suggestions I could find from experts who are supposed to know what they are talking about.

So, I've spent some time with young people, researched what others have to say about the subject, and spent some time thinking about the issues young people have to face.

Most importantly, I CARE.